COPPER-PLATE INSCRIPTIONS

BELONGING TO

THE SRI SANKARACHARYA
OF KAMKOTI-PITHA

COPPER-PLATE INSCRIPTIONS

BELONGING TO

THE SRI SANKARACHARYA OF THE KAMKOTI-PITHA

EDITED BY

T.A. GOPINATHA RAO

Gian Publishing House

29/6 SHAKTI NAGAR · DELHI-110007 · INDIA

GIAN PUBLISHING HOUSE
PUBLISHERS OF BOOKS ON HUMAN CIVILIZATION
29/6 SHAKTI NAGAR, DELHI-110007

First Reprint in India, 1986

*Printed at Goyal Offset Printers, Delhi-110035
and published by Smt. Gayatri Garg
for Gian Publishing House, Delhi-110007*

DEDICATED

WITH KIND PERMISSION

TO

HIS HOLINESS

ŚRĪ CHANDRA ŚĒKHARĒNDRA SARASVATI SVĀMI,

THE PRESENT JAGAD GURU ON THE PONTIFICAL THRONE OF

KĀÑCHI KĀMAKŌṬI PĪṬHA

OF

THE GREAT JAGAD GURU

ŚRĪ ŚAṄKARABHAGAVATPĀDĀCHĀRYA.

CONTENTS.

LIST OF ILLUSTRATIONS.

INTRODUCTION.

THE copper-plate inscriptions published in this brochure belong to the Śrī Śaṅkarāchārya Maṭha at Kumbhakōṇam. His Holiness the present Svāmi of this maṭha commanded me to edit all the copper-plate records preserved in the treasury of the maṭha and for this purpose placed for some time all the original documents at my disposal. Impressions of these grants were prepared under my supervision and their texts are edited from the paper impressions thus obtained. The records are ten in number. They consist of :—

(1) an inscription of the reign of Vijayagaṇḍagōpāladēva engraved upon a single plate which belongs to a set of which all others are lost : the remaining plate, the one available now, is the last one of the set ;

(2 & 3) two inscriptions belonging to the reign of the Vijayanagara king Vīra Nārasiṁha, the elder brother of the great Kṛishṇadēvarāya. These are complete documents ;

(4 & 5) two inscriptions of the time of Kṛishṇadēvarāya ;

(6) a fragment consisting of the first plate of a set whose other plates are lost;

(7) an inscription of the time of the Pudukkōṭṭai king Vijaya-Raghunātharāya Toṇḍaimāṇ;

(8) an inscription belonging to the reign of the Madura Nāyaka king, Vijayaraṅga-Chokkanāthayya;

(9) an inscription partly in Sanskrit, partly in Persian and partly in Telugu, a *firman* issued by the Emperor of Delhi (?); and

(10) lastly an inscription of the time of Akkaṇṇa and Mādaṇṇa, the two brāhmaṇa ministers of the Kuṭb Shāhi Sultans.

From a study of these documents it becomes patent that the Kāmakōṭi-pīṭha was situated in Kāñchīpuram till at least A.D. 1686. During the earlier part of the stay at Kāñchīpura of the *svāmis* of this line they had their *maṭha* in Vishṇu Kāñchi, on the west of the temple of Hastiśailanātha, that is, of the Varadarājasvāmin; it is only at a comparatively later period a new *maṭha* seems to have been erected in Śivakāñchi. Owing to the frequent raids of the Mussalmans on the flourishing town of Kāñchipuram, the *svāmis* were put to great inconvenience in the performance of their duties and the tradition, which is a comparatively recent one and consequently worth believing, states that Pratāpasiṁha, the Rāja of Tanjore invited the then *svāmi* of the Kāmakōṭi-pīṭha to shift his head-quarters temporarily to his capital city, Tanjore, and that the invitation was accepted and the *svāmi* immigrated into Tanjore with the golden image of Kāmākshī. The Tanjore Rāja received the *svāmi* with due honours, built for him a *maṭha* as also a temple for the Goddess Kāmākshī. Finding Kumbhakōṇam better suited to the inclinations and duties of the *svāmi*, he expressed his desire to spend his time there; a new *maṭha* was erected for him at Kumbhakōṇam on the bank of the river Kāvērī, which continues to the present time the head-quarters of the *svāmis* of the Kāmakōṭi-pīṭha; thenceforth it began to be known as the Kumbhakōṇam *maṭha* of Śaṅkarāchārya. There is a stone inscription in the *maṭha* belonging to the reign of the Tanjore king, Sarfoji, which is dated the Śaka year 1743; it states that he constructed the temple (*i.e.*, *maṭha*) for the residence of (the god) Chandramaulīśvara (the aspect of Śiva worshipped in the *maṭha*).* The second compartment in which this

---

* श्री [॥*] श्रीचन्द्रमौळेश्वरस्वामिस निवासार्थ राजश्री छत्रपति शेरफोजीमहाराज कृत आलय प्रतिष्ठा शालिवाहनशक १७४३ वृषनामसंवत्सर माघ शुद्ध पंचमी भानुवार ॥

inscription is found is said to have been erected when prince Sarfoji returned from Benares. Before that, the *pūjā-gṛiha* was in the first compartment and it is still known by the name of *paḻaya pūjai uḷḷu.*

Regarding the traditional history of the Kāmakōṭi-pīṭha, its antiquity and its superiority over the other *maṭhas* of Śaṅkarāchārya, a number of Sanskṛit works have been written ; of these the most important one is the *Guru-ratnamālikā-stōtram* by Sadāśivabrahmēndra Sarasvati with a commentary on it written by Ātmabōdhēndra Sarasvati ; both the author and the commentator were students in and eventually occupied the pontifical seat in this *maṭha.* They lived in the latter half of the 17th century A.D. Both of them have collected all the facts then available to them and put them into their works, but how far they have proved themselves critical will be shown in a separate article which I am preparing for publication elsewhere.

We learn the names of four *svāmis*, their time and their contemporaries from the records under review, namely :—

No.	Date.	Name of the Svami.	Contemporary king.
1	...	Sadāśiva Sarasvati; his disciple,	......
2	S'1429	Mahādēva Sarasvati ...	Vīra Nārasiṁhadēva.
3	S'1444	Chandraśēkhara Sarasvati (disciple of Mahādēva Sarasvati).	Krishṇadēvarāya.
	S'1450	Do.	Do.
4	S'1608	Mahādēvēndra Sarasvati (disciple of Chandraśēkhara).	Abul Hasan Kutbshah. (Akkaṇṇa and Mādaṇṇa).

From the records belonging to the Śriṅgēri Jaghir published by Mr. L. Rice in his Epigraphia Carnatica, Vol. VI, pp. 190, 206, we learn that the earliest available record found in that *maṭha* is dated A.D. 1346; whereas the earliest known document in the custody of the Kumbhakōṇam *maṭha* belongs to the year A.D. 1291. If we may judge of the relative antiquity of the two *maṭhas* from the epigraphical records existing with them at present, we are obliged to state that the Kumbhakōṇam *maṭha* seems to be older; but, I am fully awar that such a conclusion is and can not be final.

No. I.

AN INSCRIPTION OF THE REIGN OF VIJAYAGAṆḌA GŌPĀLA DĒVA.

THE subjoined inscription is engraved on the first side of a single plate which is the last one of a set, the remaining plates of which are lost. The plate is shaped exactly like those of the Vijayanagara period and has a ring hole on the curved top-portion; it had no ring when it came to me for examination.

The record is written in Grantha characters resembling those of the inscription at Śrīraṅgam of Jaṭāvarman Sundara Pāṇḍya which is edited in *Ep. Ind.* Vol. III ; (See plate facing p. 14). The language of the inscription is Sanskṛit. It records that the gift of the village of Ambikāpuram was made to the Śaṅkarāchāryasvāmi, for feeding daily 108 brāhmaṇas, by Śrī Vijaya Gaṇḍagōpāladēva, on the tenth *tithi* of the bright fortnight of the solar month Karkaṭaka of the cyclic year Khara; this day corresponded with a Monday and the nakshatra which has Mitra as its deity. Regarding the date, the Hon. Mr. L. D. Swāmikkaṇṇu Piḷḷai, M.A., LL. B., B. L., etc. has kindly supplied me with the following particulars : " Khara : Sūrya in Karkaṭaka rāśi, Monday, Śukla Dvādaśi and the nakshatra which has for its deity Mitra who presides over Anurādha. I find however that in A. D. 1291, which was Khara, on Monday, 9th July, the *tithi* ended at 53 *ghaṭikās* after mean sunrise while nakshatra Jyēshṭhā was current on the same day, having begun at 21 *ghaṭikās* after sunrise on the previous day when nakshatra Anurādha ended. I believe therefore that the date meant is Monday, 9th July 1291 A.D., and that the nakshatra for the day was Jyēshthā ; not Anurādha which is presided over by Mitra. The solar month was Karkaṭaka." The boundaries of the village Ambikāpuram are given as follows :—On the west Gṛiddhrapuram, on the east Kāñchīpuram, on the south Kaidaḍuppūr village and on the north Śiṟunanni ; it is said to have been situated on the north of the river Vēgavati in the Eyiṟ-kōṭṭam. The Śaṅkarāchāryāsvāmi, the donee of the grant, is mentioned as residing in a *maṭha* situated on the west of the temple of the god Hastiśailanāthasvāmi and that he was ever engaged in giving instruction in Vēdānta to his disciples and feeding brāhmāṇas.

The initial date of the reign of the king Vijayagaṇḍagōpāla is known from other inscriptions to be A. D. 1260. This Telugu-chōḍa king, whose political relationship with the regular line of the Chōḷas, which ended with Rājēndrachōla III, son of Rājarāja III, is unknown, was governing the Toṇḍaimaṇḍalam soon after the Paṇḍya inroads were over. The record under consideration, should have belonged to the 31st year of his reign.

In his Annual Report on Epigraphy for the year 1915, Mr. H. Kṛishṇa Śāstri writes, " It is not clearly stated in the record if the *maṭha* presided over by the Śaṅkarāchārya herein referred to was identical with the Śaṅkarāchārya *maṭha* at Conjeevaram". I fail to realise the difficulty of Mr. Śāstri in the matter of the identification of the *maṭha* mentioned in the record with that now known as the Śaṅkarāchārya *maṭha* of Conjeevaram (or Kumbhakōṇam). The main functions of the *gurus* of the Śaṅkarāchārya *maṭha* are the performance of *pūjā* to the image of Chandramauḷiśvara, *Brāhmaṇa santarpaṇa* or the feeding of the brāhmaṇas and *Advaita upadēśa* ; it is usual to refer to these three items in every letter issued from the *maṭha* to *śishyas*. All these three functions are mentioned also in the copper-plate, namely, *nityānnadāna*, *nigamānta-rahasyārtha-vivaraṇa* and the name Indumauḷi, the words *guru* and *śishya* ; all these clearly indicate the *maṭha* as that of Śaṅkarāchārya of Conjeevaram. Besides these, the copper-plate under notice is at the present time in the possession of the *svāmi* of the Kumbhakōṇam (Kāñchi Kāmakōṭi) *maṭha*, who claims through an unbroken line of succession, descent in the Kāmakōṭi maṭha. These facts appear to point clearly to the identity of the Śaṅkarāchārya *maṭha* of the inscription with the Śaṅkarāchārya *maṭha* of Conjeevaram.

The following are the names of places, etc., which occur in this document :—Ambikāpuram, Gṛiddhrapuram, Kāñchīpuram, Kaidaḍuppūr, Śirunanni, Eyiṟ-kōṭṭam, the river Vēgavati and Hastiśailam. Ambikāpuram is now known as Ambi and is situated on the west of Kāñchīpuram. Griḍdhrapuram is a meaningless translation of the Tamil name Tirupputkuḷi. Eyiṟ-kōṭṭam takes its name from the village of Eyil in the South Arcot District. Kāñchīpuram also belonged to this Kōṭṭam which was evidently divided into two halves by the river Vēgavati and in the northern of the two divisions was situated the village of Ambikāpuram. Vēgavati is the small river which passes through the town of Kāñchīpuram and empties itself into the Pālār near Timmarājanpēṭṭai. On the south of Ambi there is a village named Kadirpūr and on the north another named Śiruṇai. These may be identical with the Kaidaḍuppūr and Śiṟunanni of our record. Hastiśailam is the Attiyūr of the Vaishṇavas, that is, the present Vishṇu-Kāñchī; the temple of the God Varadarāja is situated on a raised platform which is called the *hastiśailam*. There is said to be a deserted *maṭham* near the temple of Varadarāja, which belongs to the Śaṅkarāchāryas of the Kāmakōṭi-pīṭha. But, at a later period, the *maṭha* had been shifted to Śiva-Kāñchi. In the *Maṭhāmnāya*, the name of the temple near which the Kāmakōṭi Śāradā *maṭha* was situated is said to be Satyavratakshētra, another name of Attiyūr. Hence the *maṭha* should have been situated in Vishṇu-Kāñchi and near the temple of Varadarāja-svāmi.

TEXT[1].

१. ० प्रथितात्मने । श्रीहस्तिशैलनाथस्य निलयात्

२. पश्चिमे मठे । निगमान्तरह्स्यार्थम्[2]शिष्येभ्यस्सुवित्तृण्व-

३. ते ।[।१*][3]नित्यान्नदानविधिसन्तर्प्पितात्माद्विजत्मने[4][।*]श्रीशङ्क-

४. राय्र्यगुरवे वत्सरे खरसंज्ञिते । [।२*] प्राप्ते कक्र्क[5]-

1. From inked impressions.
2. Read रहस्यार्थं
3. Metre of verses 1—12 अनुष्टुभ
4. Read सन्तर्पितात्मद्विजन्मने
5. Read कर्क

५. टकं पुण्यराशीम्[6] कमलबान्धवे [।*] मित्रदैवतन-

६. क्षत्रयुक्तायां शुक्लपक्षके । [।३*] इन्दोर्व्वारेण[7] यु-

७. क्तायां दशम्यां सुमुहूर्त्तके । प्राधिग्विधरसोपे[8]-

८. तैरन्नैरमृतसम्मितैः । [।४*] नित्यमष्टशतानाञ्च

९. तोषणाय द्विजन्मनाम् । प्राञ्चं गृद्ध्रपुरात् काञ्चीपुरात्

१०. प्रत्यञ्चमुत्तरम[9][॥५*] कैदडुप्पूरुतो ग्रामात् शिरुनन्ने-

११. श्च दक्षिणम् । वेगवत्युत्तरतटीसीमारामैकमण्डन-

१२. म् [॥६*] [10]नाळिकेरांमृपनसतालहिन्तालशोभितम् । ना-

१३. नाभूरुहवाटीनाम्[11] पुष्पसौरभवासितम् [॥७*] यैरकोष्ठिय[12]-

१४. मजन्नेन्दुमैल[13]कारुण्यरक्षितम् । अंबिकापुरनामानमग्रा[14]-

१५. मचिन्तामणीन्ददौ[15] । [।८*] [16]भुमेरस्याः प्रदानेन यावच्च-
न्द्राक्र्क[17]-

१६. योग्गतिः[18]। श्रीहस्तिशैलनिलयः प्रियतां[19] परमेश्वरः[॥९*]इत्थ-

१७. मुत्तुंगया भक्या[20] निधाय मनसिश्वरे[21] [।] देवश्रीगण्डगो-

१८. पालचोळशंकरयोगिने [॥१०*] [22]भुदानशासनं स्वस्य हस्त-

---

6. Read राशिं
7. Read इन्दोर्वारेण
8. Read प्रथग्विध
9. Read मुत्तरम्
10. Read नाळिकेराम्र
11. Read वाटीनां
12. Read यैर्कोष्ठिय
13. Read मौलि
14. Read नामानं
15. Read मणिन्ददौ
16. Read भूमेरस्याः
17. Read चन्द्रार्क
18. Read योर्गतिः
19. Read प्रीयतां
20. Read भक्त्या
21. Read मनसीश्वरम्
22. Read भूदान

Inscription of Vijaya-Gaṇḍagōpāladēva, No. I.

SCALE O. 6

T. A. GOPINATHA RAO. Half-Tone By Photo-Engraving Co., Madras.

१९. संलिखिताक्षरम् । अदादुन्नतधर्म्मस्य[23]लाभाय शुभचेतसा [॥११*]

२०. दानपालनयोर्म्मध्ये[24] दानात् श्रेयो[25]नुपा-

२१. लनम् । दानात् स्वर्गमवाप्नोति पालनादच्युतं प-

२२. दम् । [१२*]

ஸ்ரீ விஜயகண்ட கோபால தேவன்

ABSTRACT OF CONTENTS.

Śrī Śaṅkarārya-guru, residing in the *maṭha* situated on the west of the temple of Hastiśaila-nātha is expounding the Vēdānta to his disciples and is delighting in feeding daily a number of brāhmaṇas. To him, in the year Khara, when the sun was in the auspicious Karkaṭakarāśi, in the nakshatra which has Mitra as its deity, in the bright fortnight conjoined with a Monday, the tenth *tithi*, in this auspicious *muhūrtta*, for feeding sumptuously every day a hundred and eight brāhmaṇas, the village of Ambikāpuram was granted. The boundaries of this village are, on the east, Gṛiddhrapura; on the west, Kāñchīpura; on the south, Kaidaḍuppūr and on the north Śirunanni. This village is situated on the north of the river

23. Read धर्मस्य

24. Read मध्ये

25 Read दानाच्छ्रेयो

Vēgavati and is surrounded by gardens containing cocoanut, mango, jack, palmyra and other trees; is sweet-smelling with the flowers of various trees in the gardens; is situated in the Eyirkōṭṭam, and is named Ambikāpuram; by this grant (to the *svāmi*) the gratification of the god of the temple on the Hastiśaila is sought for as long as the sun and the moon last. With an intensely pious mind meditating upon god, the king, Śrī Gaṇḍagōpāla-chōḷa, (granted this village) to Śaṅkarārya-yōgi, signing this deed of land-grant with his own hand, with the expectation of obtaining great merit for making this grant. Between the protection of charity and the giving of it, the former is of greater merit than the latter; by gift (only) *svarga* (which is transient) is obtained, but protection affords abode in the imperishable region (a more desirable place than *svarga*).

No. II.

AN INSCRIPTION OF THE REIGN OF VĪRA NĀRASIṀHADĒVA ŚAKASAMVAT 1429.

THE inscription edited below is written in Nandināgari characters and in the Sanskṛit language, and is engraved upon three plates; on the first side of the first plate there is writing, but cut so faintly that to take a good impression is not easy; it begins an inscription with the usual *Śrī Gaṇādhipatayē namaḥ* and *Namastuṅga*, &c. Evidently, the engraver did not mean that the writing on this side should be taken into account. The regular beginning of the record under consideration is found only on the second side of the first plate and ends on the first side of the last plate. Though the preservation of the inscription is good, its execution is very shabby; the engraver begins it with big bold letters on the first plate and reduces the size of the letters in the subsequent plates to less than a third of those on the first side. The alphabet itself is rather peculiar and the formation of the letters somewhat curious.

The grant belongs to the reign of the Vijayanagara king, Vīra Nārasiṁhadēva, the eldest son of Narasā Nāyaka and the elder brother of the illustrious Kṛishṇadēvarāya. The genealogy of the king is, as usual, traced from the moon ; Budha, Purūravas, Āyu, Nahusha, Yayāti and Turvasu are claimed to be their ancestors by the members of the Tuḷuva dynasty, that is, the dynasty to which Vīra Nārasiṁha and Kṛishṇadēva belonged. The really historical genealogy is as follows :—

Timma, md. Dēvakī.
|
Īśvara, md. Bukkamā
|
Narasā.
|
a. by Tippāji. — Vīra Nārasiṁha.
b. by Nāgāḷa — Kṛishṇarāya.

Of these, Narasā, the father of the donor, is said to have given with due ceremonies the sixteen *mahā-dānas* in such holy places as Rāmēśvara, etc. Constructing a bridge across the Kāvērī when it was in full flood, he crossed over it and captured the town of Śrīraṅgapaṭṭaṇa and set up there a pillar of victory; then, he conquered the Chēra, the Chōḷa, the Pāṇḍya, the king of Madhura, the Turushkas and the Gajapati king. His son by Tippāji was Vīra Nārasiṁha, the donor of this and the next grant. The one under notice is dated S'1429 said to be corresponding to the cyclic year Śukla: in this year, on the Māgha-puṇyakāḷa in the month of Māgha, the king Vīra Nārasiṁha granted the villages of Elichchūr and Veṇpākkam to Mahādēva Sarasvati, the disciple of Sadāśiva Sarasvati, in the presence of the god Virūpāksha, on the bank of the river Tuṅgabhadrā. The village Elichchūr belonged to the Nīrvaḷūr-paṟṟu which was situated in the Chaṅgalipaṭṭu Sīma, belonging to the Śeṅkāṭṭu-kkōṭṭam, a sub-division of the Chandragirirājya of the Jayachōḷa-maṇḍala. Its boundaries are given as follows:—On the north, Paṇyuruṭṭi; on the south Pūḍi; on the west, Paneyūr and on the east Vaḍakkēpākkam. The boundaries of Veṇpākkam are given as follows:—On the north Paṇyuruṭṭi; on the south, Ullavūr; on the west, Vāraṇavāsi and on the east . . . At the end of the record occurs the sign-manual of the king, the word Śrī Virūpāksha, written in the Telugu-Kannaḍa characters. This copper-plate document was engraved by Vīraṇāśāri, son of Mallaṇāśāri. It is worth noting that the title of the caste is written in this and the next document as *āśāri*, the usual way in which it is pronounced at the present time, not as *āchāri*, as usual in other copperplate records.

The year S' 1429 does not really correspond to the cyclic year Śukla, which falls in the year S' 1432. The names of places, &c., which occur in this document are Jayachōḷa-maṇḍalam, Chandragirirājyam, Śeṅkāṭṭu-kkōṭṭam, Chaṅgalippaṭṭu-sīma, Nīvaḷūr-paṭṭaṇa, Paneyūru, Vaḍakkēpākkam, Paṇyuruṭṭi, Pūḍi, Elichchūru, Uḷḷavūru, Āndināḍu, Vāraṇavāsi and Veṇpākkam. Of these, Jayachōḷa-maṇḍalam is the same as the Jayaṅgoṇḍa-chōḷa-maṇḍalam of the Chōḷa period. Be it stated here that the Vijayanagara Empire, without meddling with the ancient divisions of the country which fell to its lot, retained the old divisions in almost all cases. Jayaṅgoṇḍachōḷa-maṇḍalam included the whole of Toṇḍaimaṇḍalam and perhaps a few other parts of the country adjoining it. Chandragiri is the modern town of the same name and is the headquarters of the Chandragiri Tālūkā. It was made their seat of Government by the Sāḷuvas before their usurpation of the throne of the Vijayanagara Empire; hence this division was retained as such and called the Chandragiri-rājyam and a governor was appointed to preside over it. Śeṅkāṭṭu-kōṭṭam is also an ancient name; it was, in the days of the Chōḷas, a sub-division of the Jayaṅgoṇḍachōḷa-maṇḍalam and takes its name from the village of Śeṅgāḍu in the Chingleput Tālūkā. Changalipaṭṭu-sīma is a further sub-division of the Śeṅgāṭṭu-kkōṭṭam, but is made such evidently at a later time; it is named after Chengalpaṭṭu (the Śeṅgaḻunīrpaṭṭu of the older inscriptions and the Chingleput of the present day), the head-quarters of the Tālūkā of the same name and a junction station on the South Indian Railway. Nīvaḷūr-paṭṭaṇa, Paneyūru, Elichchūru, Paṇyuruṭṭi, Vāraṇavāsi, Veṇpākkam, Uḷḷavūru and Pūḍi are the same as Nīrvaḷūr, Panayūr, Eluchchūr, Paṇruṭṭi, Vāraṇavāsi, Veṇpākkam, Uḷḷavūr and Pūṇḍi in the Conjeevaram Tālūkā.

TEXT[1].

FIRST PLATE: SECOND SIDE.

१. श्रीगणाधिपतये नमः [॥*] नमस्तुंगशिर-

२. श्चुंबिचन्द्रचामरचारवे । त्रैलोक्यनगराकार-

३. मूलस्तंभाय शंभवे । [।१*][2]हरेर्ह्लीलाव[3]तारस्य दं-

४. ष्ट्रादंडस्श[4] पातु वः । हेमाद्रिकलशो[5] यत्र धा-

---

1. From inked impressions
2. Metre of verses 1--4 अनुष्टुभ्
3. Read हरेर्लीला
4. Read दण्डस्स
5. Read कलशा

५. त्री च्छत्रश्रियं दधौ । [।२*] कल्याणायास्तु ते धाम

६. भा[त्तु ध]र्त्तुमिवापहं[6] । यद्गजोप्यगजोद्धुतं[7]

७. हरिणापि [य]दीड्यते । [।३*] तेजस्तदक्षर[8] [म]-

८. यादेव मध्यम[9]हांबुधेः । नवनीतमि-

९. वोद्धूतमहर [द्य] त्तमो महः । [।४*] तस्यासीत्तन-

१०. यस्तपोभिरतुलैरन्वास्यमानो बुधैः[10] पु-

११. ण्यैरस्य पुरूरवा भुजबलैरायद्विषां[11]

१२. [नि]घ्नतः।। तस्यायु[12]र्न्नहुषस्य नस्य पुरु-

१३. षो बुधेर्ययाति ह[13]क्षितौ ख्यातस्त [स्य]

१४. तु भूमिवासवनिभः[14] श्रीदेवयानीपतेः । [।५*][15]

१५. तदंशो[16]देवकीजानिर्महीपतिरभू[त्प]-

१६. [तिः] [।*] यशसी [तु] लुवेंद्रेषु तश कृष्णादि-

१७. वान्वयो[17]। [।६*][18]

१८. ततो भुद्बुक्कराजानामी[19]श्वर क्षितिपालकः।तत्राष्टमगुणभ्रश-[20] मौलि-

---

6. Read तद्धाम प्रत्यूहतिमिरापहम्

7. Read द्भूतं

8. Read तेजःक्षीरम

9. Read द्दैवैर्मथ्यमानान्म

10. Read रन्वर्थनामा बुधः

11. Read रायुर्द्विषां

12. Read युर्नहुषोऽस्य तस्य परु

13. Read युद्धे ययातिः

14. Other plates read तुर्वसुर्वसु-निभः

15. Metre शार्दूलविक्रीडितम्

16. Other plates read तद्वंशे देवकीजानिर्दिदीपे तिम्मभूपतिः ।

17. Other plates read यशस्वी तुलुवेन्द्रेषु यदोःकृष्ण इवान्वये ।

18. Metre of verses 6-8 अनुष्टुभ्

19. Read ततो भूद्बुक्कमाजानिरीश्वर -

20. Read अत्रासमगुणभ्रंशं मौ

First Inscription of Vīra Nārasimha, No. II.

Ib

SCALE O. 66.

A. Gopinatha Rao. Half-Tone by Photo-Engraving Co., Madras.

१९. रत्नं महीभुजां[॥७*]सच स्वादुदभूत्तस्मन नरसा[21]वनिपालकः।

२०. देवकिनंदनाकामो[22]देवाकिनंदनादभि[23][।८*] विवि॑धसुक्तैस्थ-

२१. ने[24] रामेश्वरप्रमुखे मुहुमुदितहृदयस्थाने स्थने[25]त्वधत्त य-

२२. थाविधि[26]:।बधपरिव्रतो[27]नानादानानि यो भुवि षाडश[28]त्रिभुवन-

२३. जनोद्गिनसौवर्णवानु स यथा[वि]धिः।[29][।९*][30]कावेरीमाशु

बध्वा

२४. बहळजलभरां यो विलंघ्यैव शत्रुं[नु]जीवग्राहं ग्रहि-[31]

२५. त्वा प्रथितभुजबलात्तंच रा[ज्ये] प्रहैभ्य[32][।*] [कृ] त्वा श्रिरंग-[33]

२६. पूर्वं तदपि निजवशे पट्टणं यो बभासे किर्तिस्त [भं]-[34]

२७. निखा (तं)[य*] त्रभुवनभवनं[35]स्तूयमानापदानः।[।१०*][36]चेरं

२८. चोळं च पा[ण्ड्यं] तदपि[37]च मधुरावल्लभं मानभूषा[38]वि-

२९. घ्येदग्र[39]तुरुष्कं गजपतिनूपतिं[40]चापि जित्वा तदन्य[41][।]

३०. गंगाति[म]भू [मी]प्रथमचरमदग्र तदात्तं निताख्यतः क्षो-

---

21. Read सरसादुदभूत्तस्मान्नरसा
22. Read देवकीनन्दनात्कामो
23. Read देवकीनंदनादिव
24. Read सुकृतस्थाने
25. Read मुहुर्मुदितहृदयस्स्थाने स्थाने
26. Read यथाविधि
27. Read बुधपरिवृतो
28. Read षोडश
29. Read द्रीतं स्फीतं यशः पुनरुक्त-यन्
30. Metre हरिणी
31. Read शत्रूञ्जीवग्राहं गृही-
32. Read राज्यं प्रादिश्य
33. Read श्रीरङ्ग
34. Read कीर्तिस्तम्भं
35. Read त्रिभुवनभवनस्तूयमाना-पदानः
36. Metre of verses 10-11 स्रग्धरा
37. Read पाण्ड्यं तमपि च
38. Read भूषं वी-
39. Read र्योदग्रं
40. Read नृपतिं
41. Read तदन्यान्

३१. णिपतीनां भुजमिव शिरसा शासनं यो व्यतामि[42] [॥११॥]
तिप्पाजि[43]ना-

३२. गलादेव्ये[44]कौसल्यश्रीसुमित्रयोः । देव्ये[45]रिव नृसिंहेंद्रात्त-

३३. स्माप्पंक्ति[46]र[था]दिव।[।१२*][47]वीरौ निजधना रामलक्षणा-[48]
विव नं-

३४. दना।जाता विरनसिंहेंद्र[49]कृष्णरायमहिपति[50][।][।१३*]वीरश्री

३५. नारसिंह:[51] स विजयनगरे राजसिंहासनस्थ की-[52]

३६. त्य नीत्य निरस्यन्नग[53]नळनहुषावना: प्रदता[54] [।]

३७. आसेतौरासुमेरा[55]रवनिसुरनुत स्वैरमाचाद-[56]

३८. याद्रेरापाचात्ये[57]चलांतादखिलहदयमावज्य[58]

३९. राज्यं शशास [।।१४*][59]ननादाननीन्यकाषि[तु] सदसी यश्री[60]

४०. विरूपाक्षदेवस्तने[61] श्रीकालहस्तीशतुर[62]पि नग-

---

42. आगंगातीरलङ्काप्रथमचरमभूभृत्त-टान्तं नितान्तं ख्यातः क्षोणीपतीनां स्रजमिव शिरसां शासनं यो व्यतानीत्

43. Read तिप्पाजी

44. Read देव्योः कौसल्या

45. Read देव्योरिव.

46. Read त्पङ्क्ति.

47. Read Metre of verses12-13 अनुष्टुभ् .

48. विनयिनौ रामलक्ष्मणाविव.

49. Read दनौ जातौ वीरनृसिंहेन्द्र.

50. Read महीपती.

51. Read सिंहः.

52. Read सिंहासनस्थः कीर्त्या.

53. Read नीत्या निरस्यन्नृग.

54. Read नहुषानप्यवन्या: प्रदाता.

55. Read सेतोरासुमेरो

56. Read स्वैरमाचोद

57. Read पाश्चात्या

58. Read हृदयमावर्ज्य

59. Metre of verses 14-17 स्रग्धरा

60. Read नानादानान्यकार्षीत्कनक सदसि यश्श्री

61. Read स्थाने

62. Read शितुरपि

First Inscription of Vīra Nārasimha, No. II.

IIa

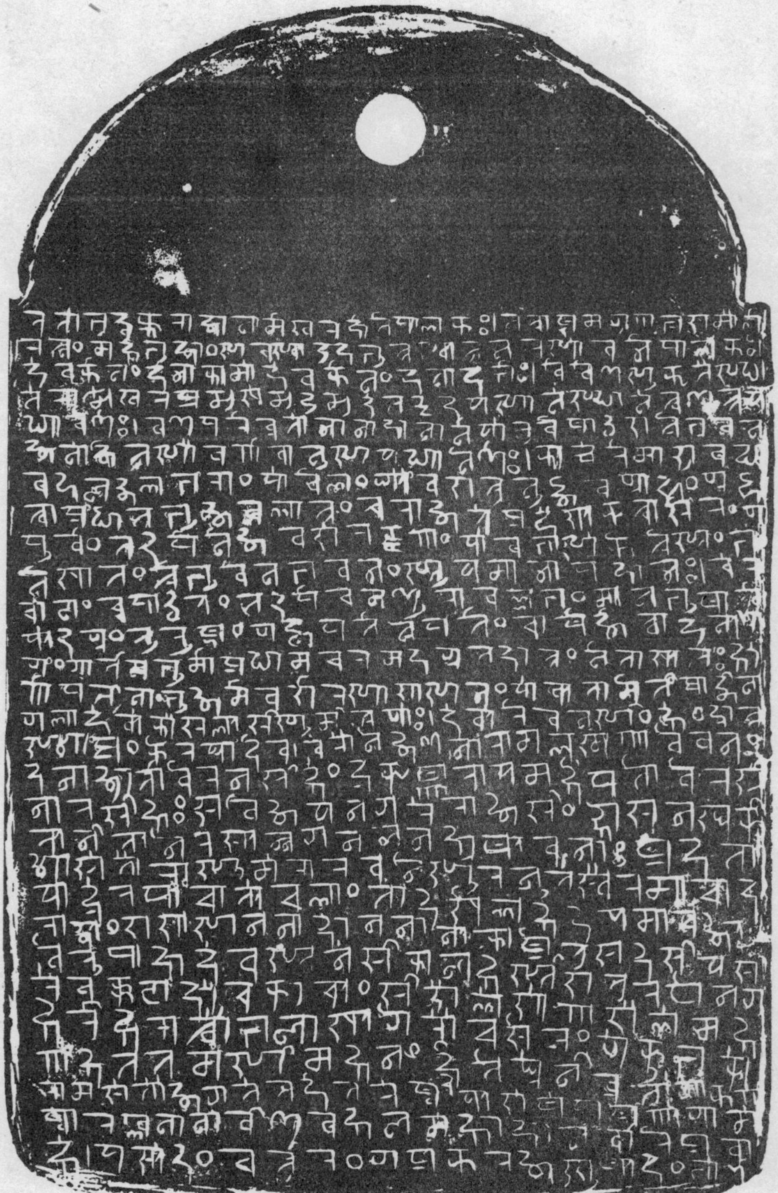

SCALE O. 66.

T. A. GOPINATHA RAO.

Half-Tone By Photo-Engraving Co., Madras.

४१. रे वक्कटाद्रौ[63]च काच्यं[64][।*]श्रीशैले शाणशैले मह-[65]

४२. हरिहरात्वौभलाख्य[66] गिरौ च श्रिरंगे कुंभको[67]-

४३. णे हृततमसी महनंदितिथे नीव्रत्तो[68][॥१५] गोक[र्णे]

४४. रामसेतौ जगति तदितरेष्वप्यशेषेषु [पु]ण्यग्रामे-

४५. ष्वार[ब्ध]नानाविधबहलमहादानवारिप्रवा-

४६. हे[69]। यस्योदंचत्तुरंगप्रकर[खुरर]जश्शुष्यदंभोधि-

SECOND PLATE: SECOND SIDE.

४७. मंत्त क्ष्माभृतपक्षचिदो[द]तरकालिशधरात्कंठिता

४८. कुंठितासि[70]।[१६*] ब्रह्माडं[71] विश्वचक्रं घटमुदितमहाभूत[कं]

४९. रत्नधेनुः[72] सप्ताभोधि ० हिरण्यश्व[73]रथमपि तुलापू-

५०. रुषं गोसहस्रं । हेमाश्वहेमगभ्रं[74]कनककरिर[थं]

५१. पंचलागल्यतनि[75] [।] धर्मैकश्वातत्रवृत्तिः प्रतिनपति[शि]

५२. रे रत्नकित्रिप्रतापः[76][१७*] राजाधिराजइत्युक्तः या राजपर-[77]

५३. मेश्वरः । मूरुरायलगंडश्च पररायभयंक्करः। [78][।१८][79]हिं

---

63. Read वेङ्कटाद्रौ

64 Read काञ्च्याम्

65. Read महति

66. Read हरे त्वौभळाख्ये

67. Read श्रीरङ्गे कुम्भघो

68. Read तमसि महानंदितीर्थे निवृत्तौ

69. Read प्रवाहैः

70. Read मग्नक्ष्माभृत्पक्षच्छिदोयत्त-रकुलिशधरोत्कण्ठिताकुण्ठिता - सीत्।

71. Read ब्रह्माण्डं

72. Read धेनुं

73. Read सप्ताम्भोधीन्हिरण्याश्व

74. Read हेमाश्वं हेमगर्भं

75. Read पंचलाङ्गल्यतानीत्

76. Read धर्म्यैकच्छत्रवृत्तिः प्रतिनृपतिशिरोरत्नकीर्तिप्रतापः ।

77. Read यो राज

78. Read भयङ्करः

79. Metre of verses 18-20अनुष्टुभ्

५४. दुरायसुरत्राणो दुष्टशार्दूलमर्दनः । वीरप्रताप इत्या-

५५. दिविशेषैरुचितैर्य्यतः।[80][।१९*] विरदेव[81] महाराज जयजीवे-

५६. ति वादिभि० अंगवंगकळिंगाद्यै राजाभिस्सेव्यते च यः[॥२०*]

५७. विज[82]नगरमध्ये रत्नसिहासनस्थः (।) जयति भूवि[83][वी]-

५८. रश्रीनृसिंहाक्षितिं[84]द्रः । नृगनहुषययातिनन्य०[न्भू[85]]-

५९. सुराणां सुरतरुरिव धीरः पुण्यकित्ति[86]प्रतापः । [।२१*][87]

६०. शकाब्दे शालिवाहस्य सहस्रेतश्च[88]तुश्शतैः । एकौन-[89]

६१. [त्रिं] शता गण्ये शुक्लनामनि वस्तरे[90][॥२२*][91]विख्याते मासि [मा]

६२. घाख्ये पुण्यकाले महोदये । तुंगभद्रानदितिरे[92]श्रीवि-

६३. रूपाक्षसान्निधौ । [२३*] परहंसपरिव्राजकाचार्यय मुमू-[93]

६४. क्षवे [।*]भस्माद्धू[94]लितगात्राय रुद्राक्षावलिधारिणे [॥२४*] शितो-[95]

६५. ष्णादिद्वंद्वदुःखव्यतिताय महान्तने[96][।*] समस्तशास्त्र-

---

80. Read र्युत:
81. Read वीरदेव
82. Read विजयनगर
83. Read सिंहासनस्थस्स जयति भुवि
84. Read क्षितीन्द्र:
85. Read नत्ययन्भूसुराणां
86. Read कीर्तिप्रताप:
87. Metre मालिनी
88. Read सहस्रेण चतुश्शतै:
89. Read एकोन
90. Read वत्सरे
91. Metre of verses 22-34½ अनुष्टुभ्
92. Read नदीतीरे
93. Read 'चार्याय मुमुक्षवे
94. Read भस्मोद्धूलित
95. Read शीतोष्णादि
96. Read व्यतीताय महात्मने

First Inscription of Vīra Nārasimha, No. II.

IIb

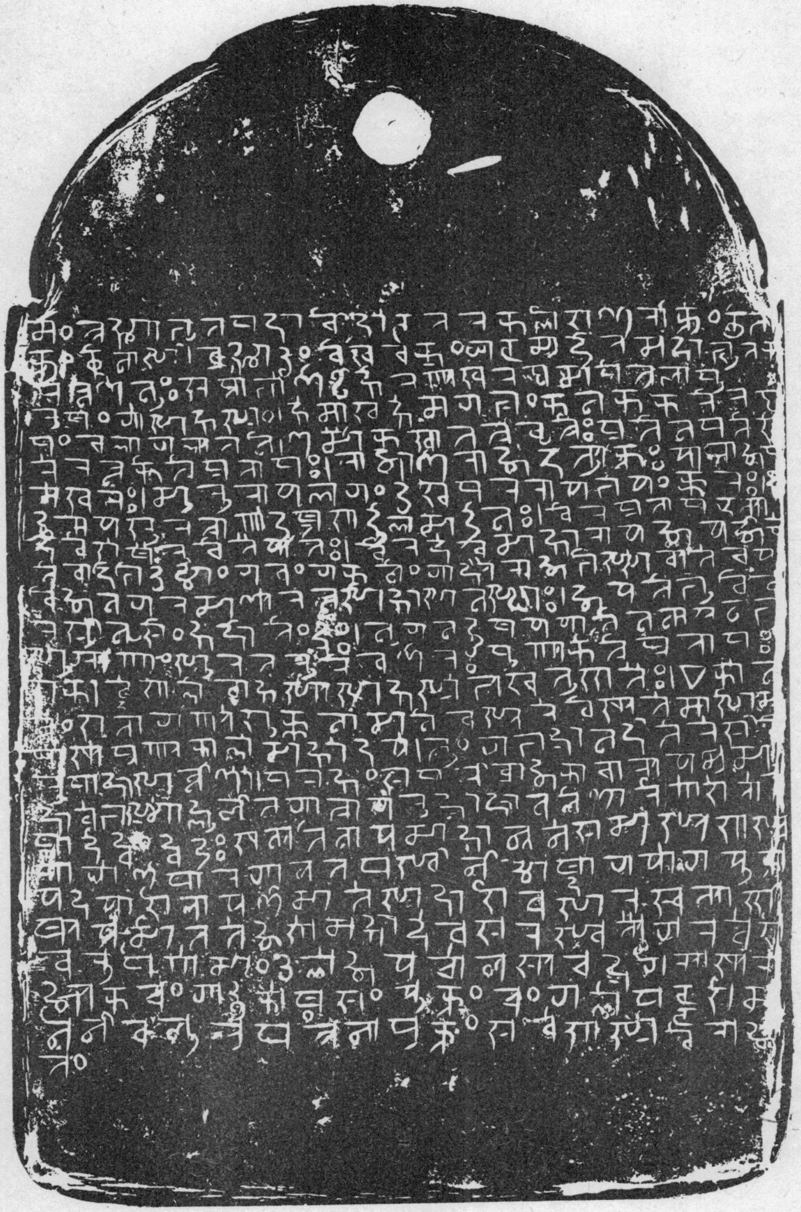

SCALE ·O. 66.

T. A. GOPINATHA RAO

Half-Tone by Photo-Engraving Co., Madras.

६६. पाथोधिपारगाय तपस्वीनी[97] [॥२५*] अष्टाग[98]योगयुक्त[ा]

६७. य दयाशिळाय धिमते[99] [।*] सदाशिवसरस्वत्याश्शि-

६८. ष्यय[100]मिततेजसे [॥२६*] महादेवसरस्वत्यै गरवे[101]शि-

६९. वरूपिणे [।*] मण्डलै[102]जयचोळस्य चद्रगिर्याख्य[103]रा-

७०. ज्यक[104] [॥२७*]चेंगाट्टुकोष्ठसंयुक्तं चंगलिपट्टशिम-[105]

७१. नि [।*] निवळूरुपत्तना[106]युक्तं सर्वशास्त्रविराज-[107]

७२. त [॥२८*]

THIRD PLATE : FIRST SIDE.

७३. पनेयुरु[108]महाग्रामातराचिं दिशिमु[109]पाश्रितं । वडक्के

७४. पक्कसुग्रामा प्रतिचिं [द्दि] शि[110]माश्रितं [॥२९*] पण्युरु[ट्टि]महा-

७५. ग्राम० दक्षिण [स्या] दिसि माश्रितं[111] [।*] पूडिनामा म [हा] ग्रादु-

७६. दीचिं दिसि माश्रितं[112] [॥३०*] एलिच्चूरिति विख्यातं ग्रामर[त्नं] प्रदि[113]

---

97. Read तपस्विने
98. Read अष्टाङ्ग
99. Read शीलाय धीमते
100. Read शिष्यायामित
101. Read गुरवे
102. Read मण्डले
103. Read चन्द्रगिर्याख्य
104. Read राज्यके
105. Read प्पट्टसीमनि
106. Read निवळूर्पत्तुना
107. Read सर्वसस्यविराजितम्
108. Read पनेयूरु
109. Read ग्रामात्प्राचीं दिश
110. Read त्प्रतीचीं दिश
111. Read ग्रामाद्दक्षिणस्यां दिशि स्थितम्
112. Read नाममहाग्रामादुदीचीं दिश
113. Read प्रदत्तवान्

७७. त्तवा [न्] एतद्गामि[114]यराज्यादिनाडुपत्तुसमन्नितं[115] । [।३१] पाण्णि-

७८. रुट्टि [म] हाग्रामादक्षिणां दिशि[116]माश्रितं । तोल्ला [वु] रुवरग्रा-

७९. मा [दु] दिच्यां दिशि सं [स्ति][117]तं [॥३२*] [वा] रण [वा] शिसुग्रामातु प्राचिं[118]दि-

८०. शिमाश्रितं[119] ।................रुनामासुग्रामा पश्चिमादिशि[120] माश्रितं [॥३३*]

८१. वेणपाक्कपुर........सर्वसस्यसमृद्धिकं । साष्टगं[121]प्र-

८२. णम ० भक्तया[122]....... ....ताम [र्णि] शुभं । [३४*] दत्त-वान्विनयान-

८३. (न) म्रः धर्म्मशिलप्रताप[123][।३४½*] यिदम [हि] तन्नपा[124]णा-मौलिरा-

८४. जकिरि[टं] ० रित[125]मणिगणानां कान्तिनिरा[126]जितांघ्रेः ।

८५. लखित...........पदै शा[127]सनं ताम्रपत्रंज ० [तु][128]भुवनसी-

---

114. Read एतद्ग्रामीय

115. Read संमन्वितम्

116. Read द्दक्षिणां दिश

117. Read दुदीच्यां दिशि संस्थितम्

118. Read सुग्रामात्प्राचीं

119. Read दिशमाश्रितम्

120. Read नामसुग्रामात्पाश्चिमां दिश

121. Read साष्टाङ्गं

122. Read न्भक्त्या ग्रामार्चन्ता

123. Read धर्मशीलप्रतापवान्

124. Read इदमहितनृपाणां

125. Read राजत्किरीटच्छुरित

126. Read कान्तिनीराजितांघ्रेः

127. Read लिखितमनघपद्यैश्शासनं

128. Read जयतु

First Inscription of Vīra Nārasiṁha, No. II

73 74 75 76 77 78 79 80 81 82 83 84 85 86 87 88 89 90

SCALE O. 66.

T. A. Gopinatha Rao. Half-Tone By Photo-Engraving Co., Madras.

८६. म्नि श्र [नृ]........क्षिति[129]द्रः । [।३५½*][130]मल्लणाशारि-
पुत्रेण वीरणाशारिसं

८७. ० ना[131][।*] लेख......वि....तदिदं ताम्रशासनं। [।३६½*]
दानपा-

८८. लनया.........[132]योनुपालनं । दानास्वम्रामा[133]वाप्नोति

८९. पालनाद[च्युतं पदं] । [३७½*] श्री

९०. श्रीविरूपाक्ष

TRANSLATION.*

ADORATION TO ŚRI GAṆĀDHIPATI.

(Verse 1). Adoration to Śambhu (Śiva) who is adorned as with a *chāmara*, with the moon that kisses his lofty head, and who is the principal pillar at the building of the city of the three worlds.

(Verse 2). May the staff-like tusk of Hari (Vishṇu) who assumed in sport the form of a boar [1] —resting on which the earth with Mount Mēru as its apex resembled an umbrella, protect you.

---

129. Read श्रीनृसिंहाक्षितीन्द्रः

130. Metre मालिनी

131. Read संज्ञिना

132. Read पालनयोर्मध्ये दाना-च्छ्रेयो

133. Read दानत्स्वर्गमवाप्नोति

* Translations of verses 1, 3, 5 to 8, 10 to 17, are of Dr. Hultzsch; those of verses 2, 4 and 9 are of Messrs. Butterworth and Venugopala Chetti.

1. This refers to the boar incarnation of Vishṇu.

(Verse 3). May that lustre (Gaṇēśa)—which dispels the darkness of obstacles, and which, though it has the head of an elephant (*gaja*), was born from the mountain-daughter (*Agajā*) and is worshipped even by Hari (Vishṇu),—produce happiness.

(Verse 4). From the milky ocean which was churned by the gods arose like fresh butter the luminary (moon) by which darkness is dispelled [1].

(Verse 5). The son of this (moon) was Budha, whose name (was made) true to its meaning by his unequalled austerities. In consequence of his pious deeds (he obtained a son), Purūravas. (The son) of him, who destroyed the life (*āyus*) of his enemies by the strength of his arm, was Āyus. His (son) was Nahusha. His (son) was Yayāti, who was fierce in battle (and) famed on earth. (The son) of this husband of the glorious Dēvayānī was Turvasu, who resembled the Vasus.

(Verse 6). In his race shone king Timma, whose wife was Dēvakī, (and) who was famous among the princes of Tuḷuva just as Kṛishṇa (shone) in the race of Yadu.

---

1. The allusion is to the churning of the ocean of milk by the gods. The moon is supposed to have then sprung from it.

(Verse 7). From him was born king Īśvara, whose wife was Bukkamā (and) who was the fearless and virtuous crest-jewel of kings.

(Verse 8). From this lovely son of Dēvakī was born king Narasā, just as Kāma from (Kṛishṇa) the son of Dēvakī.

(Verse 9). Rendered famous for various good deeds, with a delighted mind, surrounded by wise men, he again and again made the sixty kinds of gift according to prescribed rules, at Rāmēśvaram and every other holy place, thus increasing (*lit.* rendering superfluous) his great renown which was sung by the denizens of the three worlds.

(Verse 10). Resplendent was he, who quickly bridged the Kāvērī [1] (though) it consisted of a rapid current of copious water, crossed over it, straightway captured alive in battle with the strength of his arm the enemy, brought his kingdom and (the city of) Śrīraṅgapaṭṭaṇa [2] under his power and set

1. Śrīraṅgapaṭṭaṇa, *vulgo* Seringapatam, which, later on, became the capital of the Maisūr Oḍeyars and of Ṭipu is situated on an island of the Kāvērī.

2. Literally '(that compound ending in) paṭṭaṇa, the first member of which is Śrīraṅga.' (On similar expressions see Hultzsch's South-Indian Inscriptions, Vol. 1, p. 166, note 6).

up a pillar of fame,—his heroic deeds being praised in the three worlds, (which appeared to be) the palace (of his glory).

(Verse 11). Having conquered the Chēra, the Chōḷa, the proud Pāṇḍya (who was) the lord of Madhurā, the brave Turushka, the Gajapati king and others, he, who was exceedingly famed from the banks of the Gaṅgā to Laṅkā and from the slopes of the eastern to those of the western mountain, spread his command like a garland on the heads of kings.

(Verses 12 and 13). Just as Rāma and Lakshmaṇa (were born) to Daśaratha by his queens Kausalyā and the glorious Sumitrā, (thus) two brave (but) modest sons, prince Vīra Nṛisiṁha and prince Kṛishṇarāya, were born to king Nṛisiṁha by his queens Tippāji and Nāgaḷa (respectively).

(Verse 14). The illustrious Vīra-Nārasiṁha, seated on a jewelled throne at Vijayanagara, surpassing in fame (and) wisdom Nṛiga, Naḷa, Nahusha and (all) other (kings) on earth, being voluntarily praised by the Brāhmaṇas (and) winning all hearts —ruled the kingdom from (Rāma's) Bridge to (Mount) Sumēru and from the mountain of the east to the western mountain.

(Verse 15). He performed various gifts at the Golden Hall,[1] at the shrine of the holy Virūpākshadēva,[2] at the town of the holy lord of Kāḷahasti,[3] on Vēṅkaṭādri,[4] at Kāñchī, at Śrīśaila,[5] at Sōṇaśaila[6] at the sacred (city of) Harihar,[7] at Ahōbaḷa,[8] at Saṁgama, at Śrīraṅga[9] at Kumbhaghōṇa,[10] at the sinless *tīrtha* of Mahānandi[11] (and) at Nivṛitti.

(Verse 16). The streams of water (poured out) at copious great gifts of various kinds, which

---

1. *Kanaka-sadas* is a synonym of Kanaka-sabhā, 'the Golden Hall' at the temple of Chidambaram in the South Arcot District.

2. This is the old name of the Pampāpati temple in Hampe.

3. This town is now the residence of a Zemindar in the North Arcot district.

4. Vēṅkaṭādri, 'the hill of Veṅkaṭa' is the name of the holy mountain (Tirumalai) near Tirupati in the North Arcot district.

5. In the Karnūl district.

6. Śōṇaśaila or Śōṇāchala, 'the red mountain' is the hill of Tiruvaṇṇāmalai in the South Arcot district.

7. This town is situated in the Mysore territory on the frontier of Dharwad.

8. In the Karnūl district.

9. This is the great island temple near Trichinopoly.

10. In the Tanjore district.

11. In the Karnūl district.

he performed at Gōkarṇa[1] at Rāma's Bridge, and at all other sacred places in the world, frustrated the eagerness of (Indra) the bearer of the thunderbolt, who was ardently rising to clip the wings[2] of the mountains, which were immersed in the ocean, that was being dried up by the dust of the hoofs of the troops of his prancing horses.

(Verse 17). He performed (the gifts of) a mundane egg, a wheel of the universe, a pot containing the (five) elements, a jewelled cow, the seven oceans, a tree and a creeper of paradise, a celestial cow of gold, an earth of gold, a horse-chariot of gold, the weight of a man (in gold), a thousand cows, a horse of gold, a (golden vessel called) *hēmagarbha*, an elephant-car of gold, and five ploughs.

(Verses 18-21). This king who is distinguished by the *birudas* Rājādhirāja, Rājaparamēśvara, Mūru-rāyala-gaṇḍa, Para-rāyabhayaṅkara, the

---

1. In the North Kanara district.

2. Following a suggestion of Paṇḍit Lakshmaṇāchārya of Bangalore, I separate *paksha-chhida-udyatara-Kuliśadhara-utkaṇṭhita*. Indra's eagerness was frustrated, as the water poured out at the king's donations refilled the ocean, which the dust of his army had dried up, and thus saved the mountains from persecution.

Sultan among the Hindu Rājas, Dushṭa-śārddūla-marddana, Vīra-pratāpa etc., is adored by the kings of the Aṅga, the Vaṅga, the Kaliṅga etc., countries, saying 'O Vīradēva, Mahārāja! Be you victorious, May you live long.' Vīra Nārasiṁhamahārāya, who is as munificient as the *kalpaka* tree to the brāhmaṇas, who is valorous and whose fame is unsullied, shines on the jewelled throne in the middle of the city of Vijayanagara excelling even Nṛiga, Nahusha and Yayāti.

(ABSTRACT OF THE CONTENTS OF THE REMAINING PORTION OF THE DOCUMENT).

Ll. 60-69. In the Śālivāhana Śaka year one thousand four hundred and twenty-nine in the (cyclic) year Śukla, and on the auspicious occasion of the Māgha-mahōdaya in the month Māgha, the king granted in the presence of (the god) Virūpāksha on the bank of the river Tuṅgabhadra the villages of Elichchūr and Veṇpākkam to Mahādēva Sarasvati, disciple of Sadāśiva Sarasvati, who is a Paramahaṁsa-Parivrājakāchārya seeking liberation; whose body is smeared with ashes, and adorned with rudrāksha-garlands; who is a great person, who is unaffected by the effects of cold and heat; who has studied thoroughly all the *śāstras* and who is also a *tapasvi* (a doer of *tapas* or penance); who has attained the eight yōga sādhanas, namely *yama*, *niyama*, etc., who is full of grace and is of bright intellect ; and resembles Śiva himself.

L. 69. The village of Elichchūr is situated in the Nīrvaḷūr-paṟṟu, in the Changalipaṭṭu-sīmē of the Cheṅgāṭṭukōṭṭam, which is a sub-division of the Chandragiri-rājya situated in the Jayachōḷa-maṇḍala ; it is situated on the east of the village of Paneyūr ; on the west of the village of Vaḍakkē-pakkam ; on the south of the village Paṇyuruṭṭi and on the north of Pūḍi. The village of Veṇpākkam is situated in the same *paṟṟu*, *kōṭṭam*, *nāḍu* and *rājya* as Elichchūr and its boundaries are :—

It is situated on the south of the great village of Paṇṇiruṭṭi, on the north of the superior village of Uḷḷavūru, on the east of the good village of Vāraṇa-vasi and on the west of the good village of . . . . This village is full of all sorts of vegetation. The charitable and famous king having prostrated in the *sāshṭāṅga* fashion, with love and veneration granted this village.

May this copper-plate document of the king Vīra-Nārasiṁha, whose feet are made resplendent by the contact of the collection of gems in crowns of rival kings, be victorious on this earth ; this copper-plate grant was engraved by Vīraṇāśāri, son of Mallaṇāśāri.

INSCRIPTION OF VĪRA NĀRASIṀHADĒVA.

As between gift and protection, the latter is more meritorious for by the former one attains *svarga* (which is not permanent) whereas by the latter, eternal bliss. Śrī Virūpāksha.

No. III.

A SECOND INSCRIPTION OF THE REIGN OF VĪRA NĀRASIṀHA OF THE SAME YEAR.

THIS record is exactly similar to the previous one even in the matter of the date: on the same occasion as in the former case, the village of Kuḍiyāntaṇḍalam was granted to the same *Svāmi*, Mahādēva Sarasvati, the disciple of Sadāśiva Sarasvati.

The village Kuḍiyāntaṇḍalam is said to have been situated on the Vamāvanpaṭṭu (Viṇṇavampaṭṭu?) of the Kāliyūrkōṭṭam, in the Valakūru Sīmā, situated in the Kachchināḍu, a sub-division of the Paḍavīḍu-rājya of the Jayachōḷamaṇḍala. It was bounded on the north by Kaḷakāṭūru; on the east by Śuriṭṭilūṟu; on the south by Śitteleppākkam and on the west by Kūtan-tāṅgal.

Of the names of places mentioned in this document we have already identified in dealing with the previous record Jayaṅgoṇḍaśōlamaṇḍalam.

Paḍavīḍu-rājyam takes its name from the village of Paḍavīḍu. Velkūru-sīmā is so named after Velkūru in the Chittoor Taluka; [Viṇṇa]-vambaṭṭu is in the Pōḷūr Tālūkā. Kāliyūr-kkōṭṭam is a division of the Chōḷa period. There are two Kaḷakāṭūrus, of which one is in the Conjeevaram Tālūkā of the Chingleput District, which does not appear to be the one that is referred to here; the other is in the Palmanēr Tālūkā of the N. Arcot district and this is perhaps the village which the inscription means to refer. Śuriṭṭilūru and Śitteleppākkam have to be identified with the villages of Śuruṭṭal and Śittelep-pākkam in the Arcot Tālūkā. Kachchināḍu and Kūtamtāṅgal have to be looked for also in the N. Arcot district, though the *List of Villages* does not give their names in it. Kuḍiyāntaṇḍalam now goes by the name of Kuṇḍiyāntaṇḍalam and is situated in the N. Arcot district. The *maṭha* still owns some lands in this village.

TEXT [1].

FIRST PLATE FIRST SIDE.

१. श्रीगणाधिपतय[2] नमः[॥*]नमस्तुगशीरचुं-[3]

२. बिचंद्रचामरचारवे । त्रैलोकानगराकारमु-[4]

---

1. From inked impressions.
2. Read पतये
3. Read नमस्तुङ्गशिरश्चुम्बि
4. Read त्रैलोक्यनगराकारमूल

Second Inscription of Vīra Nārasiṁha, No. III.

Ia

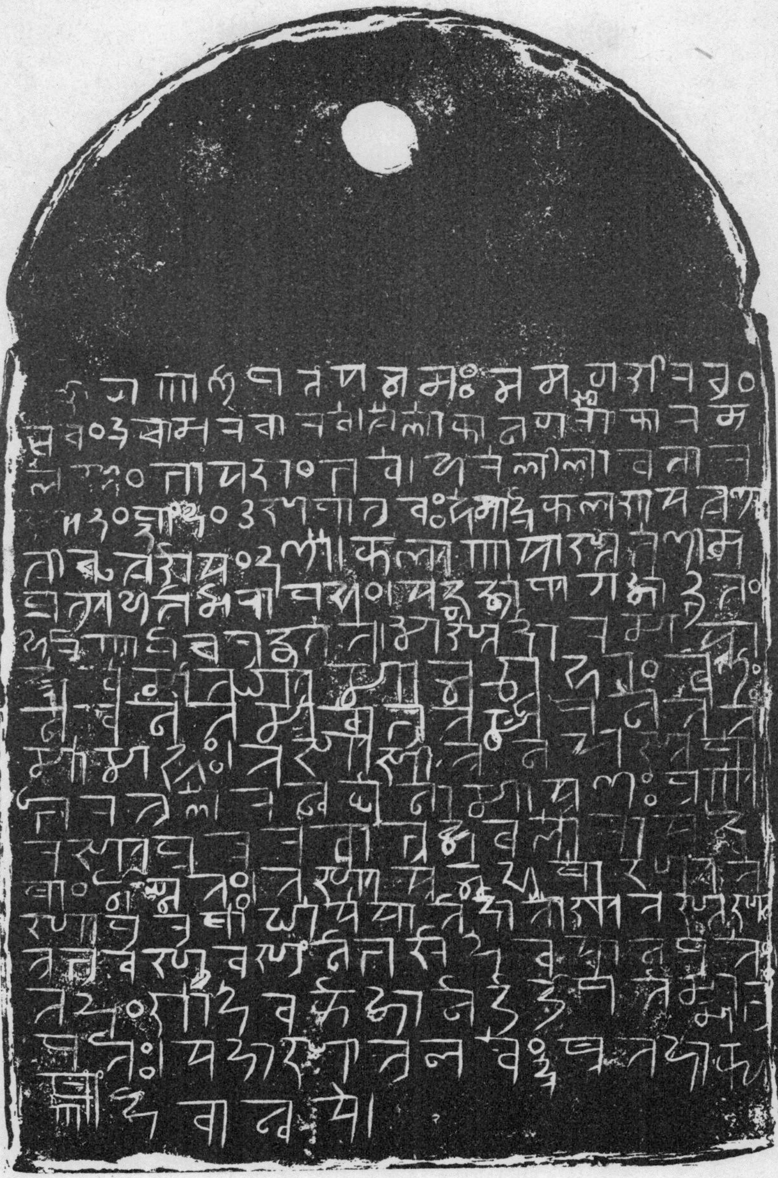

SCALE O. 66.

T. A. GOPINATHA RAO. Half-Tone by Photo-Engraving Co., Madras.

३. लस्तंभाय शंभवे । [।१*][5] हरे लीला[6]वतार-

४. स्य दंष्ट्रादंड[7] स पातु वः[।*] हेमाद्रिकलशः यत्र धा-

५. त्री च्छत्रश्रियं दधौ । [।२*] कल्याणायस्तते धाम[8]

६. प्रत्यु[9]हातिमिरापहं । यद्गजोप्यगजोद्भुतं[10]

७. हरिणापि च पूज्यते । [।३*] अस्ति क्षिर[11]मया-

८. हेवेर्मथ्यमान[।*]न्महांबाधिः[12][।*]

९. नवनीतमिवो[13]भूतमपनीतत-

१०. मो महः । [।४*] तस्यासीत्तनयस्तपो-

११. भिरतुलैरन्वर्थनामा पुधः[14] पुण्यै-

१२. रस्य पुरूरवा भुजबलौ[15]रायु [द्वि]-

१३. षां निघ्नतः। तस्यायु न[16]हुषोस्य त-

१४. स्य पुरुषो [धेये] याति[17] क्षितौ ख्यातस्तस्य

१५. तु भुवसु[18]वसुनिभ [३*] श्रीदेवयानपतेः[19] [।।५*][20]

१६. तदंशो[21] देवकीजानि दिदीपे[22] तिम्मभू-

---

5. Metre of verses 1-4 अनुष्टुभ्

6. Read हरेर्लीला

7. Read दण्डस्स

8. Read कल्याणायास्तु तद्धाम

9. Read प्रत्यूह

10. Read द्भूतं

11. Read क्षीरमया-

12. Read देवैर्मथ्यमानान्महाम्बुधेः

13. Read द्भूतं

14. Read बुधः

15. Read बलैरायु

16. Read तस्यायुर्नहुषोस्य

17. Read परुषो युद्धे ययातिः

18. Read तुर्वसुर्वसुनिभ

19. Read देवयानीपतेः

20. Metre शार्दूलविक्रीडितम्

21. Read तद्वंशे

22. Read दिदीपे

१७. पतिः। यदासी तुळवेंद्रेषु[23] तदा[24] कृ-
१८. ष्णा[25] इवान्वये । [।६*][26]

FIRST PLATE SECOND SIDE.

१९. ततोभूद्बुक्कराजानामीश्व[27]रक्षितिपालकः। तताष्टमगुणभ्रंश[28][मौ]
२०. लि[र]त्नं महीभुजां । [।७*] स च स्वा[29]उदभूत्तस्मात् नरसो-
वनिपालक[30][:।*]
२१. देवकीनंदना कामो[31] देवकीनंदनादिभिः[32] । [।८*] विविध-
सुकृतै स्था-
२२. नै[33]रामेश्वरप्रमुखे मुहुर्मुदितहृदयस्थाने स्थानत्वध-
२३. त्त यथाविधिः[34] । बुधपरिवृतो नानादानानि यो भुवि षाड-
२४. श त्रिभवनजनोद्गीतसौवर्णवानु स यथावि-
२५. धिः।[35] [।९*][36][का] वेरीमाशु बध्वा बहळजलभरां यो विलंघ्यै-
२६. व [श] तुनुं[37] जिविग्राह ग्रहित्वा[38] प्राथतभुजबलांत्त-
२७. च राज्य[39] प्रदिश्य [।*] कृत्वा श्रीरंगपूर्वं तदपि निजवशे

---

23. Read यशस्वी तुळुवेन्द्रेषु
24. Read यदोः
25. Read कृष्ण इवा
26. Metre of verses 6-8 अनुष्टुभ्
27. Read बुक्कमाजानिरीश्वर
28. Read अत्रासमगुणभ्रशं
29. Read सरसादुद
30. Read नरसावनिपालकः
31. Read नन्दनात्कामो
32. Read नन्दनादिव
33. Read सुकृतस्थाने
34. Read स्थाने स्थाने त्वधत्त यथाविधि
35. Read षोडश त्रिभुवनजनोद्गीतं स्फीतं यशः पुनरुक्तयन्
36. Metre हरिणी
37. Read शत्रूञ्जीव
38. Read गृहीत्वा
39. Read राज्यं

Second Inscription of Vīra Nārasimha, No. III.

Ib

SCALE O. 66.

T. A. GOPINATHA RAO. Half-Tone by Photo-Engraving Co., Madras.

२८. पट्टणं यो बभासे कीर्त्ति[40]स्तंभं नखातं त्रिभवन[41]भ-
२९. वनं स्तू[42]यमानापदानः। [।१०*][43]चेरं चाळंच पाड्यं तद-[44]
३०. पि च मधुरावल्लभं मानभूषावि[र्ये]दग्रं[45] तुरुष्कं
३१. गेजपतिनृपार्ति[46]चापि जित्वा तदन्य[ान् *][।]आगंगातीरभूमा-
३२. षथमचरमदग्रतदात्तं[47] निता[न्तं*] ख्यातः क्षोणि-
३३. पतिनां भुजमिव शिरसा[48] सासनं यो व्यतानि[49] [।।२१*]
३४. तिप्पाजिनागलादेव्ये[50] कौसल्यं[51] श्रीसुमित्रयोः । दे-
३५. व्यरिव[52] नृसिंहेंद्रात्तस्माप्पक्तरथादि वी[53][।।१२*][54] रौ निह-
धनौ[55] राम-
३६. लक्ष्मणाविव नंदनौ [।] जातौ वीरनसिंहेंद्र[56]कृष्णरायम-
३७. हीपति[57] । [।१३*] वीर[श्रीनार*] सिं[ह]ः स विजयनगरे
राजसिंहासन-
३८. स्थः(।) कीर्त्य[।*] नीत्य[।*] निरस्य नृग[58]नळनहुषानप्यव-
न्य[।*]ः प्र-

---

40. Read बभासे कीर्ति
41. Read निखाय त्रिभुवन
42. Read भवनस्तूयमाना
43. Metre of verses 10-11 स्रग्धरा
44. Read चोळं च पाण्डयं तमपि
45. Read वल्लभं मानभूषं वीर्योदग्रं
46. Read गजपतिनृपर्ति
47. Read भूमिप्रथमचरमभूभृत्त-टान्तं
48. Read क्षोणीपतीनां स्रजमिव शिरसां
49. Read शासनं यो व्यतानीत्
50. Read तिप्पाजीनागलादेव्योः
51. Read कौसल्या
52. Read देव्योरिव
53. Read त्पङ्क्तिरथादिव
54. Metre of verses 12-13 अनुष्टुभ्
55. Read वीरौ विनयिनौ
56. Read नृसिंहेन्द्र
57. Read पती
58. Read निरस्यन्नृग

३९. दाता । आसेतोरासुमेरोरपतिसुरनुत[59]स्वैरमाचो-

४०. दयाद्रेरापाश्व[ा*]त्य[ा*] [च]ळांता[द*] खिलहदपमावज्य[60]-

४१. रा[ज्य]शशास्त्र[61]। [१४*][62] ननादान्[न्य]काषी[63] [त्]कनक
[सदसि यः*] श्रीवि-

४२. [रूपाक्ष] देवस्तने श्र[64]काळहस्तीशतुरपि[65] नगरे वे-

४३. क्कताद्रौ च काच्यं[66][:] श्रीशैलै शोणशैले मह[ति*]हरि-

४४. हरे त्वैाभळाख्ये गिरौ च श्रीरंगे कुंभकोणे ह-

४५. ततमसि महानंदितीर्थे निव्रतौ[67][॥१५*]

SECOND PLATE FIRST SIDE.

४६. गोकंर्णे[68] रामसेतौ जगति[तदि*] तरेष्वप्यशेषेपु[69][पु]ण्य-
ग्रामेष्वा-

४७. रब्धनानाविधबहळमहादानवारिप्रवाहे । पस्ये[70]दं-

४८. चत्तुरंगप्रकरखुर[रज]श्शुष्यदंभोधिवांत्त[71] (:) क्ष्मा-

४९. भतषक्षाचिदौवत्तरकलिशधरोत्कुंठिता कंठिता-

५०. सीत[72] । [।१६*] ब्रह्मांडं विश्वचक्रं घटमुदितमहाद्भुत[73]-

---

59. Read रवनिसुरनुतस्स्वैर
60. Read हृदयमावर्ज्य
61. Read राज्यं शशास
62. Metre of verses 14-17 स्रग्धरा
63. Read नानादानान्यकार्षी
64. Read स्थाने श्री
65. Read हस्तीशितुरपि
66. Read वेङ्कटाद्रौ च काञ्च्यां
67. Read तीर्थे निवृत्तौ
68. Read गोकर्णे
69. Read प्यशेषेषु
70. Read प्रवाहैः । यस्यो
71. Read वान्त
72. Read भृत्पक्षच्छिदोद्यत्तरकुलिशधरोत्कण्ठिता कुण्ठितासीत्
73. Read भूतकं

Second Inscription of Vīra Nārasiṁha, No. III

IIa

SCALE O. 66.

T. A. GOPINATHA RAO.

Half-Tone By Photo-Engraving Co., Madras.

५१. कं रत्नधेर्नुः सप्ताभोधि[74][न]हिरण्य[।*]श्वरथमपि[तु] [ला*]

५२. पुषं[75]गोसहस्रं । हेमाश्वं हेमगर्भं[76]कनककरि-

५३. रथं पंचलांगल्यतानी[द् *] धर्मैकश्चातन्नृत्वात्तिः[77]

५४. प्रनिन्नपतिशरेरत्नकीत्ति[78]प्रतापः । [।१७*] राजाधिराज

५५. (इराज) इत्युक्तः यो राजपरमेश्वरः । मूरुरायल-

५६. गंडश्च पररायभयंक्करः[79] । [।१८*][80] हिंदुरायशुरत्रा-[81]

५७. णो [दु] ष्टशार्दूलमर्दनः । वीरप्रताप इत्यादिविशेषै-

५८. रुचितै [र्यो] तः । [82][।१९*] वीरदेव महाराय जयजीवेति

५९. वादिभिः । अङ्गवङ्गकाळिंगाद्यैराजाभिस्सेव्य-

६०. ते च पः।[83][।२०*] विज[य*]नगरमध्ये रत्नसिहासन[84]स्थः (।) ज-

६१. यति भुवि [स*] वीरशीनसिह[85]क्षितीन्द्रः । नृगनहुषययाति-

६२. नन्यय[न][86]भूसुराणां सुरतरुरिव धीरः पुण्यकी-

६३. त्ति[87]प्रतापः । [।२१*][88]शकाब्दे शालिवाहस्य सहसेृभ्य-[89] श्चतुश्श-

---

74. Read रत्नधेनुं सप्तांभोधीन्

75. Read पूरुषं

76. Read हेमगर्भे

77. Read धर्म्यैकच्छत्रवृत्ति:

78. Read प्रतिनृपतिशिरोरत्नकीर्ति

79. Read भयङ्करः

80. Metre of verses 18-20 अनुष्टुभ्

81. Read सुरत्ताणो

82. Read र्युत:

83. Read य:

84. Read सिंहासन

85. Read श्रीनृसिंह

86. Read ययातीनन्वयन्

87. Read कीर्ति

88. Metre मालिनी

89. Read सहस्रेण चतु

६४. तैः । एकोनत्तृंश[90]ता गण्ये शङ्कनामनि वस्तरे[91][॥२२*][92]
विख्या-

६५. तै मासि माघाख्ये पुण्यकाले महोदये [।*] तुगभद्रा[93]न-

६६. दीतीरे श्रीविरूपाक्षसन्निधौ । [२३*] परहंसपरिव्राजका[या]

६७. [र्या]य[94]मुमुक्षवे [।] भस्मोद्धूलितगात्राय रुद्राक्षावलि-

६८. धारिणे [॥२४] शीतोष्णादिद्वंद्व (द्वं) दुःख(ा)व्यतीताय
महाम्तने ।[95]

६९. समस्तस्तास्त[96]पाथोधि पारगाय तपस्विने । [।२५*] स्मष्टां[97]

७०. गयोगयुक्ताय दयाशीलाय धमते[98][।] सदाशिव-

७१. सरस्वत्यै[99]श्शिष्य[।*] यामिततेजसे[॥ २६*] महे [दे*]-[100]
वसरस्वत्यै गुरवे शिवरूपिणे ।

SECOND PLATE: SECOND SIDE.

७२. मण्डले जयचोळस्य पडवीडुसुराज्यक[101][॥ २७*] काश्चि-
नाडुसमा-

७३. युक्तं वलका [टू] रुसीमनि । वमावं ० पत्तुनागुक्तं[102] कालि-
युरुकोष्ठसन्वानितं[103] । [।२८*]

---

90. Read त्रिंशता

91. Read वत्सरे

92. Metre of verses 22-31½ अनुष्टुभ्

93. Read तुङ्गभद्रा

94. Read र्याय

95. Read महात्मने

96. Read शास्त्र

97. Read अष्टाङ्ग

98. Read धीमते

99. Read सरस्वत्या

100. Read महादेव

101. Read राज्यके

102. Read युक्तं

103. Read कालियूर्कोष्ठसंयुतम्

Second Inscription of Vīra Nārasimha, No. III.

SCALE O 66.

T. A. GOPINATHA RAO. Half-Tone by Photo-Engraving Co., Madras.

७४. कलकाटूरुसुग्रामा[द्दक्षिण]स्यां दिशि स्थितं । शुरिट्टिल्लुरुम-[104]

७५. हाग्रामा प्रतीच्यां दिशि[105]माश्रितं । [।२९*] शित्तेलेपाकसुग्राम-
दुत्तरस्यादि-[106]

७६. शि स्तितं[107][।]कु [तं] ताम्रलुम्र[।*]मापुत्रस्यां दिशिमु[108]पा-
श्रितं । [।३०*] नाळिकेरा-

७७. म्रपनशताळहिंत्ताळ[109]शोभितं । सर्व [स*]स्य(।) [स*]मृद्धया
च राजमानं

७८. शुभान्वितं । [।३१*] कुडियांतण्डलाख्यातं ग्रामरत्नं प्रदत्तवा-

७९. ०[110] [।३१½*] यिदम [हि][111] तनपाणामौलिराज्रकि [री*]
टस्फुरितमणिगणानां

८०. का [न्ति] नीराज[112]तांघे: । लसतमनघयक्षशासनं नम्रपात्रं[113]

८१. जयतु भुवनसीम्नि श्रिन्रसिंहक्षितिंद्र:[114]। [।३२*] [115]मल्लणा-
शारिपुत्रेण (।)

८२. वीरणाशारिसंहि[116]ना । लिखितं लब्ध [वि*] [धे] न तदिदं
ताम्रशा-

---

104. Read शुरिट्टिलूर्महा
105. Read त्प्रतीच्यां दिश
106. Read दुत्तरस्यां दि
107. Read स्थितम् •
108. Read पूर्वां दिश
109. Read म्रपनसताळहिन्ताळ
110. Read प्रदत्तवान्
111. Read इदमहितनृपाणां मौलि-
राजत्किरीट
112. Read नीराजिताङ्घ्रेः
113. Read लिखितमनघपद्यं शा
सनं ताम्रपत्रं
114. Read श्रीनृसिंहक्षितीन्द्रः
115. Metre मालिनी
116. Read संज्ञिना

८३. सनं। [।३३*] दानपालनयोम्नध्ये दानाश्रेयो[117]नुपालनं । दा-
नास्वग्र-[118]

८४. मवाप्नोति पालनादच्चु[119]तं पदं । [।३४*][120]

८५. श्रीविरूपाक्ष

ABSTRACT OF CONTENTS.

(The translation of verses 1-21 is the same as in the previous document).

Verses 22-37½. In the Śaka year of the Śālivāhana (era) one thousand four hundred and twenty-nine, in the (cyclic) year Śukla, and on the auspicious occasion of the Māghamahōdaya in the month Māgha, the king granted in the presence of (the god) Virūpāksha, on the bank of the river Tuṅgabhadrā, the village of Kāvāntaṇḍalam which is situated in the Kāliyūrkōṭṭam in Vāma.... paṭṭu (Viṇṇavanpaṭṭu?), of the Kaḷakā[ṭu]ru-sīmā, belonging to the Kachchināḍu of the Paḍaivīḍu-rājya, a sub-division of the Jayachōḷamaṇḍala, to Mahādēva Sarasvati, disciple of Sadāśiva Sarasvati, (with his praises as in the previous document). The village of Kāvāntaṇḍalam is situated on the

117. Read मेध्ये दानाच्छ्रेयो

118. Read त्स्वर्ग

119. Read दच्युत

120. Metre of verses 33-34 अनुष्टुभ्

south of the good village of Kaḷakāṭūru, on the west of the great village of Suriṭṭilūru, on the north of the village of Sitteleppākkam and on the east of Kūtantāṅgal. This village looks bright with the plenty of cocoanut, mango, jack, palmyra trees and all other vegetation.

(As in the previous document it is stated here that the engraving was done by Vīraṇāśāri, son of Mallaṇāśāri and then follows the verse extolling the merits of protecting a gift and the sign-manual of the Vijayanagara kings, Srī Virūpāksha).

Chinnādēvī-Ammanavaru. Kṛishṇadēvarāyaru. Tirumaladēvī-Ammanavaru:
Bronze: Veṅkaṭēśa Temple, Tirumala, Tirupati.

No. IV.

AN INSCRIPTION OF THE REIGN OF KṚISHṆADĒVARĀYA, ŚAKA SAMVAT 1444.

THIS inscription is also engraved on three plates; the writing begins on the second side of the first plate and ends on the first side of last one. The preservation and the execution of the writing are good. The alphabet of the record is Nandināgari and the language is Saṅskṛit. The sign-manual the words Śrī-Virūpāksha, occurring at the end of the record is, as usual, written in Telugu-Kannaḍa characters.

The inscription belongs to the reign of the king Kṛishṇadēvarāya and is dated the Śaka year 1444, which corresponded with the (cyclic) year Svabhānu. On the *gō-dvādasi tithi* in the bright half of the month Mārgaśīrsha, in this year, the king granted the villages of Poḍavūr and Kāṭṭup-pattu to Chandrachūḍa Sarasvati, the disciple of Mahādēva Sarasvati; the grant was made on the bank of the river Kṛishnavēṇi and at the time of the grant the name of the village Poḍavūr was changed into Kṛishnarāyapuram. The Yati Chandrachūḍa Sarasvati is distinctly mentioned as a resident of Kāñchīpuram. The two villages mentioned are said to have been situated in Nīrvaḷūrnāḍu, a sub-division of Seṅgāṭṭukkōṭṭam, in the Mudukāṭṭupparṟu, which belonged to the Chandragirirājyam. The boundaries of Poḍavūr are given as follows:—

On the west of this village is situated the village of Seṅgōḍai;

on the north	Kandūr;
on the east	Akkāḷivēlūr; and
on the south	Śēndamaṅgalam

and those of Kāṭṭuppattu are:—

On the west of this village is situated the village of Śiruvāgai;

on the east	Parundūr;
on the north	Kōṭṭayākkam; and
on the south	Śiruvaḷūr.

At the end of this copper-plate grant, it is stated that it was composed by Sabhāpati and engraved on copper-plates by Vīraṇāchāri, son of Mallaṇa. The historical information supplied in this record is identical with that obtained from the others belonging to this dynasty of Vijayanagara king and therefore need not be reiterated here or hereafter.

Seal belonging to No. II. Same Size.

Seal belonging to No. IV. Same Size.

Seal belonging to No. V. Same Size.

The Svāmi, Chandrachūḍa Sarasvati, should be the same as Chandraśēkhara Sarasvati of the list supplied by the *Gururājaratnamālikā* (as also of No. V below) and whose date as calculated from the list also comes to be S' 1429-1445. The word *gō-dvādaśi* occurs in other inscriptions also but it is not evident what the importance of this *dvādaśi* is.(1) The following are the places mentioned in the record : Chandragirirājyam, Mudukaṭṭupparru, Śeṅgāṭṭukkōṭṭam, Nīrvaḷūrnāḍu, Poḍavūr, Śeṅgōḍai, Kandūr, Akkāḷivēlūr, Śēndamaṅgalam, Śiruvāka, Parundūr, Kōṭṭavākkam, Śiruvaḷūr, Kāñchīpuram and the Kṛishṇavēṇi river. The two villages of Poḍavūr and Kāṭṭuppattu being said to be situated in the Nīrvaḷūrnāḍu, they and the villages bounding them should be looked for in the Conjeevaram Tālūka in which Nīrvaḷūr is situated. Poḍavūr is in the same Tālūkā and goes by the same name even now; but the name Kāṭṭuppattu does not occur in the *List of Villages*; it is perhaps to be identified with Kāṭṭēripattu. The villages Kandūr,

---

(1) In the inscription No. 53 belonging to the Koppa Tālūkā of the Kadūr District, Mysore State, this is called *gōvatsa-dvādaśi*. The name *gō-dvādaśi* occurs also in an inscription of the reign of the Āy or Vṛishṇi Chief, Vikramāditya Varaguṇa, A. D. 868. (See *Trav. Arch. Series*, Vol. I, p. 192).

Akkāḷivēlūr, Śēdamaṅgalam (evidently Śēndamaṅgalam), Parundūr, Kōṭṭavākkam, Śiruvāka and Śiruvaḷūr are to be identified with Kandūr, Śandavēlūr, Śēndamaṅgalam, Parundūr, Kōṭṭavākkam, Śiruvākkam and Śiruvaḷūr,—villages which are situated in the Conjeevaram Tālūkā of the Chingleput District. I am unable to identify Mudukkāṭṭupparru and Śeṅgōḍai. The river Krishṇavēṇī is the same as the modern Krishṇā river.

TEXT [1].

FIRST PLATE SECOND SIDE.

१. श्रीगणाधिपतये नमः [॥*] नमस्तुंगशिरश्चुंबिचंद्रचामरचा[र]

२. वे । त्रैलोक्यनगरारंभमूलस्तंभाय शंभवे । [।१*] हरेर्ह्ली[2]-लावराह-

३. स्य दंष्ट्रादंडःस पातु वः । हेमाद्रिकलशा यत्र धात्री च्छत्राश्रियं [द]-

४. धौ । [।२*] कल्याणायास्तु तद्धाम प्रत्यूहतिमिरापहं । यद्गजो-प्यगजो-

५. [द्भू]तं हरिणापि च पूज्यते । [।३*] अस्ति क्षीरमयाद्देवैर्मध्य-मानान्मु[3]०-

६. बुधेः । नवनीतमिवोद्भूतमपनीततमो महः । [।४*][4] तस्या-सीत्तन[य]-

---

1. From inked impressions.
2. Read लीला
3. Read मथ्यमानान्महा
4. Metre of verses 1—4 अनुष्टुभ्

७. स्तपोभिरतुलैरन्वर्ध[5]नामा बुधः (।) पुण्यैरस्य पुरूरवा भुजब-

८. ० रायुद्वि[6]षां निघ्नतः । तस्यायुर्नहुषोस्य तस्य परुषो युद्धे यया-

९. [ति][7]क्षितौ (।) ख्यातः[8]स्तस्य तु तुर्वसुर्वसुनिभश्री[9]देवयानी-
पते[10] । [।५*][11] त[द्वं]-

१०. शे देवकीजानिद्दि[12]दीपे तिंमभूपतिः । यशस्वी तुलुवेंद्रेषु
यदो[:]

११. कृष्ण इवान्वये । [।६*][13]ततोभूद्बुक्कमाजानिरीश्वरक्षिति-
पालकः । अ-

१२. त्रासमगुणभ्रंशं मौळिरत्नं महीभुजां । [।७*]सरसादुदभूतस्मांन[14]
[र]-

१३. सावनिपालकः । देवकीनंदनः कामो देवकीनंदनादिव । [।८*]
कावे[री]-

१४. माशु बध्वा बहळजलरया[15]यो विलंघ्यैव शत्रुं (।) जीवग्राहं प्र-

१५. हीत्वा समित[16]भुजबलात्तंच राज्यं तदीयं । कृत्वा श्रीरङ्गपूर्वं

१६. तदपि निजवसे[17]पट्टणं यो बभासे (।) कीर्तिस्तंभं निखाय त्रि-
भुवन-

---

5. Read रन्वर्थ
6. Read लैरायुर्द्विषां
7. Read तिः
8. Read ख्यातस्तस्य
9. Read निभश्श्री
10. Read पतेः
11. Metre शार्दूलविक्रीडितम्
12. Read जानिर्दि
13. Metre of verses 6-8 अनुष्टुभ
14. Read त्तस्मान्नर
15. Read रयां
16. Read सामिति
17. Read वशे

१७. भवनस्तूयमानापदाना[18] । [।९*][19]चेरं चोळं च पाण्ड्यं तदपि (तमपि) च मधुरावल्ल-

१८. भं मानभूषं(।) त्रीयोंदग्रं तुरुस्कं[20]गजपतिनृपतिं चापि जित्वा त-

१९. दन्यान् । आगंगातीरलंकाप्रथमचरमभूभृ [त्त]टांतं नितांतं

२०. ख्यातः क्षोणीपतीनां स्रजमिव शिरसा[21]शासनं यो व्यतानी[22] । [।१०*] विवि-

२१. धसुकृतोद्देमे[23]रामेश्वरप्रमुखे मुहुर्मुदितहृदय[१*]स्थाने स्थाने व्य-

२२. धत्त यथाविधि । बुधपरिवृतो नानादानानि यो भुवि षोडश त्रि-

२३. भुवनजनोद्गीतं स्फीतं यशः पुनरुक्तयन् । [११*][24]तिप्पाजी-नाग-

२४. ळादेव्यो[25]काशल्या[26]श्रीसुमित्रयोः । देव्योरिव नृसिंहेंद्र तस्मा-त्पङ्क्ति[27]-

२५. रथादिव । [।१२*][28]वीरौ विनयनौ[29]रामलक्ष्मणाविव नंदनौ । जातौ वी-

२६. रनृसिं[हें*]द्रकृष्णरायमहीपती । [।१३*] वीरश्रीनारसिंहः स त्रिजयन-

२७. गरे रत्नसिंहासनस्थाः[30](।)कीर्त्या नीत्या निरस्य[31] नृगनळन-

---

18. Read दानः

19. Metre of verses 9 10 स्रग्धरा

20. Read तुरुष्कं

21. Read शिरसां

22. Read व्यतानीत्

23. Read द्दामे

24. Metre हरिणी

25. Read देव्योः

26. Read कौसल्या

27. Read द्रात्तस्मात्पंक्ति

28. Metre of verses 12-13अनुष्टुभ्

29. Read विनयिनौ

30. Read सनस्थः

31. Read स्यन्नृग

First Inscription of Kṛishṇadēvāraya. No. IV.

Ib

SCALE O. 6.

T. A. GOPINATHA RAO. Half-Tone By Photo-Engraving Co., Madras.

SECOND PLATE FIRST SIDE.

२८. हुषानप्यवं[32]न्यामधन्यान् । आसेतोरासुमेरोरवनिसुरनतस्वै[33]-

२९. रमाचोदयाद्रेरापाश्चात्याचलंता[34]दखिलहृदयमावर्ज्य राज्यं श-

३०. शास । [।१४*][35] नानादानां[36]न्यकार्षीकि[37]नकसदशि[38]यः श्री-
विरूपाक्षदेवस्था-

३१. ने श्रीकाळहस्तीशितुरपि नगरे वेंकटाद्रौ च कांच्यां [।*] श्री-
शैले शोण-

३२. शैले महति हरिहरे होबळे संगमे च श्रीरंगे कुंभघोणे हततम-

३३. सि महानंदितीर्थे निवृ[त्तौ] । [।१५*] गोकर्णे रामसेतौ जगति
तदितरेष्व-

३४. प्यसेषेषु[39] पुं[10]ण्यस्थानेष्वालब्ध[41]नानाविधबहुळमहादानवारि

३५. प्रवाहैः । यस्या[42]दंचत्तुरंगप[43]करखुररजशु[14]ष्यदंबोधिमग्नः[45]
क्ष्मा-

३६. भूप्रहाहिदाद्दरकुलिशधरोःकंटिता कुंटिताभूत्[46] । [।१६*]
ब्रह्मांडं

---

32. Read प्यवन्या
33. Read नुतस्वै
34. Read चलान्ता
35. Metre of verses 14-17 स्रग्धरा
36. Read दानान्य
37. Read कार्षीत्क
38. Read सदसि
39. Read प्यशेषेषु
40. Read पुण्य
41. Read ष्वारब्ध
42. Read यस्यो
43. Read प्रकर
44. Read रजश्शु
45. Read भोधिमग्न
46. Read भृत्पक्षच्छिदोद्यत्तरकुलिशधरोत्कण्ठिता कुण्ठिताऽभूत्

३७. [वि]श्वचक घटमदि[47]तमहाभूतकं रत्नधेनुं सप्तांबोधिं (भोधिं)
ष कल्प-

३८. [क्ष ?][18]तिरुहलतिके कांचनी[49](क ।)कामधेनुं[।*] स्वर्ण-
क्ष्मां यो हिरण्याश्वरथ-

३९. मपि तुलापूरुषं गोसहस्त्रं (।) हेमाश्वं हेमगर्भं कनककरिरथ[50]

४०. पंचलांगल्यतानीत् । [।१७*] प्राज्यं प्रशास्य निर्विघ्नं राज्यं
द्यामिव शा-

४१. सितुं । तस्मिन्गुणेन विख्याते क्षितेरिंद्रे दिवं गते । [।१८*][51]
ततोप्यवार्यवी-

४२. र[52]श्रीकृष्णरायमहीपतिः । बिभर्ति मणिकेयूरानिर्विशेषं मही[53]

४३. भुजे । [।१९*] कीत्या[54]यस्य समंततः प्रसृतया विश्व[55]
रुचैक्यं व्रजेदि-

४४. त्याशंक्य पुरा पुरारिरभवद्धाळे[56]क्षणः प्रायशः । पद्माक्षो-

४५. पि चतुर्भुजोजनि चतुव[57]क्त्रोभव(ः।)पद्मभूत्का[58]ळी खड्गमथा-[59]

४६. द्रमाच्च[60]कमलं वीणां च वाणी करे । [।२०*][61]शत्रूणां वास-
मेते ददत

---

47. Read चक्रं घटमुदित
48. Read क्षिति
49. Read काञ्चनीं
50. Read रथं
51. Metre of verses 18-19अनुष्टुभ्
52. Read र्यश्श्री
53. Read महीं
54. Read कीर्त्या
55. Read विश्वं
56. Read त्फाले
57. Read चतुर्वक्त्रो
58. Read त्पद्मभूःकाली
59. Read मथा
60. Read रमा च
61. Metre शार्दूलविक्रीडितम्

First Inscription of Kṛishṇadēvarāya, No. IV.

IIa

28 29 30 31 32 33 34 35 36 37 38 39 40 41 42 43 44 45 46 47 48 49 50 51 52 53 54

SCALE O. 6.

T. A. GOPINATHA RAO. Half-Tone by Photo-Engraving Co., Madras.

४७. इति रुषा किंनु सप्तांबुराशी[62]नानासेनातुरंगत्रुटितव-
४८ सुमतीधूळिकापाळिळकाभि:[63] । सशोष्य[64] स्वैरमेतत्प्रातिनिधि-
४९. जलधिश्रेणिका यो विधत्ते (।) ब्रह्मांडस्वर्णमेरुप्रमुखनि-
५०. जमहादानतोयैरमेयैः ।[२१*][65]मद्दत्तामर्धिसार्त्थे[66]श्रियमिह
५१. सचिरं[67] भुंजतामित्यवेत्य प्रायः प्रत्युह[68]हेतोस्तपनरथ-
५२. [ग]तेरालयं देवतानां । तत्तद्दिग्जैत्रवृत्या[69]पि च बिरुदु[70]प-
५३. दैः रंकितांस्तत्रतत्रैः[71] (।) स्तंभांजातप्रतिष्टान्व[72]तनुत भुवि
५४. [यो भ] भृदभ्रंकषाग्रान्[73] । [२२*] कांचीश्रीशैले[74]शोणा-
चलकनकसभा-

SECOND PLATE: SECOND SIDE.

५५. वेंकटाद्रिःप्रमुखे[75]ष्वावर्त्यावर्त्य सवष्व[76]तनुत विधिवद्भूय[स्य][77]
५६. श्रेयसे यः । देवस्थानेषु तीर्थेष्वपि कनकतुलापूरुषादी-
५७. नि नानादानान्येयों[78]पदानैरपि सममखिलैरागमोक्ता-

---

62. Read राशीन्नाना
63. Read पाळिकाभि:
64. Read संशोष्य
65. Metre of verses 21-23 स्रग्धरा
66. Read मर्थिसार्थाश्रिय
67. Read सुचिरं
68. Read प्रत्यूह
69. Read वृत्त्या
70. Read बिरुद
71. Read दैरङ्कितांस्तत्र तत्र
72. Read स्तभाञ्जातप्रतिष्ठान्व्य
73. Read भूभृदभ्रंकषाग्रान्
74. Read श्रीशैल
75. Read द्रिप्रमुख्ये
76. Read सर्वेष्व
77. Read द्भूयसे
78. Read न्येवो

५८. नि तानि । [२३*]रोषक्तप्रतिपार्थिवदंड(।)शेष[79]भुज[80] क्षितिर-

५९. क्षणशौंड[81] । भाषेगेतप्पुवरायरगंड(।)स्तोषक्कदार्त्थिषु[82]यो

६०. रणचंडः । [२४*][83]राजाधिराज इत्युक्तो यो राजपरमेश्वरः। मू-

६१. रु[84]रायरगंडाश्व[85] पररायभयंकरः । [२५*][86]इंदुरायसुरत्राणो

६२. दुष्टशार्दुल[87]मर्दनः । वीरप्रताप इत्यादिबिरुदैरुचितै-

६३. र्युतैः।[88][।२६*] आलोकय महाराय जय जीवेति वादिभिः। अं-

६४. गवंगकालिंगाद्यै राजभिः सेव्यते च यः । [।२७*] स्युत्यौ-

६५. दार्यसुधीभि [सौ।][89]विजयनगरे रत्नसिंहासनस्थः (।) क्ष्मा-

६६. पालन्[90]कृष्णरायक्षितिपतिरधरीकृत्य नीत्या नृगादी-

६७. न् । आपूर्वाद्रेरथास्तक्षितिधरकटकादाच हेमाचला-[91]

६८. तादासेतोरर्थिसाथ[92]श्रियमिह बहळीकृत्य कीर्त्या समिंधे । [।२८*][93]

६९. शालिवाहननिर्नीते[94]शकाब्दे गणिते क्रमात् । सहस्रेण चतुः- श्चत्वा-[95]

---

79. Read दण्डश्शेष
80. Read भुजः क्षिति
81. Read शौण्डः
82. Read दर्थिषु
83. Metre दोधक
84. Read मूरुराय
85. Read गंडश्च
86. Metre of verses 25-27 अनुष्टुभ्।
87. Read शार्दूल
88. Read युतः
89. Read स्तुत्यौदार्यस्सुधीभिस्स
90. Read पालान्
91. Read चलां
92. Read सार्थ
93. Metre स्रग्धरा
94. Read निर्णीते
95. Read चतुश्चत्वा

First Inscription of Kṛishṇadēvarāya, No. IV.

IIb

SCALE O. 6.

A. Gopinatha Rao.

Half-Tone By Photo-Engraving Co., Madras.

७०. रिंशता च चतुःशतैः[96] । [।२९*][97]स्वभानुवत्सरे मासि मार्ग-
शीर्षकनामनि[।*]

७१. कृष्णवेणीतटे शुद्धगोद्वादश्यां महातिथौ । [।३०*] मह[98]देव-
सरस्वत्याः

७२. [99]शिवचेतसे । व्याख्याताखिलशास्त्राय विख्याताय महात्मने
[।३१*]

७३. कांचीपुरनिवासाय मायावादांबुधीदवे[100] । चंद्रचूडसरस्वत्यै

७४. यतिराजाय धीमते । [।३२*] चंद्रगिर्य्याख्यराज्यस्थं मूतुका-
[ट्टा]ख्यपतु-[101]

७५. गं। चेंकाट्टुकोट्टकांशस्थं निव्त्रळूर्नाडुके स्थितं । [।३३*]
चेंगोडेग्रामका-

७६. त्प्राच्यं कांतूरोरपि दक्षिणं [।*] ग्रामादक्काळिवेलूरुनामकाद-

७७. पि पाश्चिमं । [।३४*] सेदमग[102]लकात् ग्रामादुत्तरस्यां दिशि
स्थितं । कृष्ण-

७८. रायपुरं चेति प्रतिनामसमाश्रितं । [।३५*] प्राक्तनी[103] पोड-
वूरा-

७९. रव्यां[104] माश्रितं ग्राममुत्तमं । सर्वमान्य[105]चतुःसी[106]मासंयु-

८०. तं च समंततः । [।३६*] निधिनिक्षेपपाषाणसिद्धसाध्यज-

---

96. Read चतुश्शतैः

97. Merte of veres 29-43 अनुष्टुभ्

98. Read महादेव

99. The word "शिष्याय" must be inserted before the word "शिवचेतसे"

100. Read बुधीन्दवे

101. Read पत्तु

102. Read मङ्गलकाद्

103. Read प्राक्तनीं

104. Read ख्यामाश्रितं

105. Read सर्वमान्यं

106. Read चतुस्सीमा

THIRD PLATE : FIRST SIDE.

८१. लानिनतः[107] [।*] अक्षिण्यागामिसंयुक्तमेकभोग्यं सभूरुहं ।
[।३७*] विस

८२. यप्रषिशाभोग्यं[108] क्रमादाचंद्रतारकं [।*] दानस्याधमनस्यापि
विक्र-

८३. यस्यापि चादितः[109] [॥३८*] परीतः प्रयतैस्निग्धै[110] पुरो-
हितपुरोगमैः [।*] वि-

८४. विधैर्विबुधैः श्रौतप्रतीकै[111]रधिकैर्गिरा । [।३९*] कृष्णदेव-
महारायो मा-

८५. निनीयो[112] मनस्विनां । साहिरण्यपया[113]धारापूर्वकं दतवा[114]
[न्] [॥४०*]

८६. एत [द्ग्रा] मिप[115]राज्यादिनाड्यकोठसमन्वितं । शिरुत्राकम-
दाग्रामात् प्रा-

८७. च्यां दिशि विराजितं । [।४१*] परुंद्रभिधा[ग्रा] मा[116]प्रतिचिं
दिशिमाश्रितं[117] । कोट्ट-

८८. वाकाद्वपग्रामा [त्] द[118]क्षिणस्यां दिशि स्थितं । [।४२*] शिरु-
वळुरुस[119]ग्रामा

107. Read लान्वितम्

108. Read शिष्यप्रशिष्यकैर्भोग्यं

109 Read चोचितम्

110. Read प्रयतैस्स्निग्धैः

111. Read पथिकै

112. Read ननीयो

113. Read पयो

114. Read दत्तवान् मुदा

115. Read एतद्ग्रामीय

116. Read भिधाद्ग्रामात्

117. Read प्रतीचीं दिश

118. Read ह्वयग्रामाद्

119. Read वळूरुसु

First Inscription of Kṛishṇadēvarāya, No. IV.

IIIa

SCALE O. 6.

T. A. Gopinatha Rao. Half-Tone by Photo-Engraving Co., Madras.

८९. दुदीचिं[120]दिशमाश्रितं । काट्टपट्टभिधानं च ग्रामरत्नं प्रदत्तवान् । [।४३*]

९०. तदिदमवनीवनीपगवितितु[121]धरा[य]स्य कृष्णरायस्य । शा-

९१. सनमुरुकविवैभवनिवह(निवह)निदानस्य भूरिदानस्य । [।४४*][122]

९२. कृष्णदेवमहारायशासनेन सभा [पतिः । अभा*] णीं[123]मृदुसं- दर्भं तदिदं तां-

९३. ब्र[124]शासनं । [।४५*] [25]कृष्णदेवमहारायशासनान्मल्लणात्मज- [ः।*] त्वष्टा

९४. श्रीवीरणाचार्यो [व्य] लखत्तांब्र[126]शासनं । [।४६*] दान- पालनयोर्मध्ये

९५. दानाच्छ्रेयोनुपालनः[127] [।*] दानात्स्वर्गमवाप्नोति पालनाद- च्युतं प-

९६. दं । [।४७*] स्वदत्ताद्रि[128]गुणं पुण्यं परदत्तानुपालनं । परदत्तापहारेण

९७. स्वदत्तं निष्फलं भवेत् । [।४८*] स्वदत्ता[129]परदत्तां वा यो हरेत वसुंध-

---

120. Read दुदीचीं

121. Read वनीपकवितति

122. Metre गीत्यार्या

123. Read णीन्मृदु

124. Read ताम्र

125. Metre of verses 45-50 अनुष्टुभ्

126. Read व्यलिखत्ताम्र

127. Read च्छ्रेयोऽनुपालनम्

128. Read द्द्विगुणं

129. Read स्वदत्तां

९८. रां । षष्टि र्वष[130] सहस्राणि त्रिष्टायां[131] जायते किमि[132] ।[।४९*]
एकैथ[133]भगि-

९९. ती[134]लोके सर्वेषामेव भूभुजां । त[135] भोज्या न करग्राह्य[136]विप्रद-

१००. त्ता वसुंधरा । [।५०*] सामान्यो य[137]धर्मसेतुर्नृपाणां काले
काले पाल-

१०१. नीयो भवद्भिः । सर्वानेतान्भाविनः पार्थिवेंद्रान्भूयो भूयो या-

१०२. चते रामचद्रः[138] । [५१*][139]

१०३. श्रीविरूपक्ष[140]

TRANSLATION.

(Verses 1 to 18) are the same as in II and III.

(Verses 18 and 19). When, having ruled his great kingdom without obstacles, this Indra of the earth, who was famed for virtue, had gone to heaven, as if it were in order to rule heaven (too), the illustrious king Krishṇarāya, whose valour was irresistible, bore the earth on his arm like a bracelet of jewels.

---

130. Read षष्टिं वर्ष
131. Read विष्ठायां
132. Read क्रिमिः
133. Read एकैव
134. Read नी लोके
135. Read न भोज्या
136. Read करग्राह्या
137. Read सामान्योऽयं
138. Read रामचन्द्रः
139. Metre शालिनी
140. Read श्रीविरूपाक्ष

(Verse 20). It was probably through fear, lest everything should assume an identity of lustre from his fame, which was spread everywhere, that, of old, Śiva adopted a (third) eye on his forehead (as a distinguishing mark), Vishṇu, four arms, Brahmā four faces, Kāḷi a sword, Rāma a lotus, and Vāṇi a lute in her hand.

(Verse 21). Was it through anger, because they gave refuge to his enemies, that he dried up the seven oceans with the clouds of the dust of the earth, which was split by the horses of his numerous armies, and of his own accord created in their stead masses of oceans by the immeasurable waters (poured out) at his great gifts, which consisted of a mundane egg, a Mēru of gold, etc.?

(Verse 22). It was probably in order to obstruct the path of the chariot of the sun in the sky, with the view that the crowds of suppliants should enjoy as long as possible the riches given by him, that this lord of the earth set up in every part of the earth firmly fixed pillars, which were marked with (an account of) his expeditions for conquering each quarter and with (his) surnames (*biruda*) and the tops of which touched the clouds.

(Verse 23). Again and again, for the sake of supreme happiness, he performed according to rule those various gifts which are prescribed in the holy books, *viz.*, the weight of a man in gold, &c., together with all minor gifts, at Kāñchi, at Śrīśaila, at Śōṇāchala, at the Golden Hall, on Vēṅkaṭādri and at all other temples and bathing places.

(Verses 21 to 26). Some of his surnames (*biruda*) were :—The angry punisher of rival kings ; he whose arms resemble (the coils of the serpent) Sēsha ; he who is versed in protecting the earth ; the destroyer of those kings who break their word ; he who satisfies suppliants ; he who is fierce in war ; the king of kings and the supreme lord of kings ; the destroyer of the three kings (of the south) ; he who terrifies hostile kings ; the Sultan among Hindu kings ; he who crushes the wicked like tigers.

(Verse 27). He is served by the Aṅga, Vaṅga, Kaliṅga and other kings, who speak thus :—"Look (upon me), Oh great king ! Be victorious ! Live (long) !"

(Verse 28). Seated on a jewelled throne at Vijayanagara, king Kṛishṇarāya, whose liberality was worthy to be praised by the learned, having surpassed Nṛiga and other kings in wisdom, and having bestowed abundant riches on all suppliants on earth, was resplendent with fame from the eastern mountain to the slopes of the mountain of the west and from the mountain of gold (Mēru) to (Rāma's) Bridge.

No. V.

ANOTHER INSCRIPTION OF THE REIGN OF KṚISHṆADĒVARĀYA, ŚAKA SAMVAT 1450

THE inscription edited below also belongs to the reign of Kṛishṇadēvarāya but is dated six years after his first grant to the maṭha, No. IV above. In the meantime the donee of No. IV above was no more and was succeeded by Sadāśiva Sarasvati and to this latter the present grant is made. The inscription recording the grant is in Nandināgari characters and in the Sanskṛit language. In the year S' 1450 corresponding to the cyclic year Virōdhi, on a Sunday, which was the Paurṇimā tithi (full-moon) in the month Vaiśākha and was coupled with the nakshatra Viśākha, the king Kṛishṇadēvarāya granted the village of Udayambākkam to Sadāśiva Sarasvati, the disciple of Chandraśēkhara Sarasvati (Chandrachūḍa of No. IV above) : the ceremony of making the *dāna* took place in the presence of the god Virūpāksha, on the bank of the river Tuṅgabhadrā; at that time the name of the village was changed into Kṛishṇarāyapura. The village of Udayambākkam is said to have been situated in the Paḍaviḍurājyam, a sub-division of the Jayachōḷamaṇḍalam, in the Tirukkāḷikan-iraṇḍārru-parru, belonging to the Kaḷattūr-kōṭṭam, in the Śrīvalimalainādu of the Chaṅgalipaṭṭu-sīmā; and it was situated on the bank of the Kshīranadi. The boundaries of the village are given as follows:—

On the west was situated the village of Praḷḷyanūr;

on the north	Maṇappākkam;
on the east	Kaḷattūr, and
on the south	Puṇyappaṭṭu.

In the document it is stated that Sabhāpati was the composer of it and that it was engraved upon copper-plates by Vīraṇāchāri, son of Mallaṇāchāri; and at the end the sign-manual of the king, the words Śrī Virūpāksha, is written in large sized Telugu-Kannaḍa characters.

The following note regarding the date was kindly supplied to me by Mr. L. D. Swamikkannu Pillai:—

"S'. 1450, Virōdhi, Vaiśākha paurṇimā, Viśākha nakshatra, Sunday. The tithi and nakshatra in question ended on Monday 4th May, 1528 A. D. at 23 ghaṭika and 7 ghaṭika, respectively after mean sunrise. As the tithi and nakshatra must have commenced at or about the corresponding parts of the previous day, Sunday, the date referred to is therefore Sunday, 3rd May, 1528 A.D."

The names of places occurring in this inscription are---Udayambākkam, Paḍavīḍu-rājyam, Jayaṅgoṇḍachōḷamaṇḍalam, Tirukkāḷigan-raṇḍāṟṟupaṟṟu, Kaḷattūr-kōṭṭam, Śrīvalimalaināḍu, Chaṅgalipaṭṭu-sīmā, Praḷḷayanūr (?), Maṇappākkam, Kaḷattūr, Puṇyappaṭṭu and Kshīranadi. Of these Tirukkālingan-raṇḍāṟṟu-paṟṟu seems to have received its name from Tirukkāḷikkāḍu (?) in the Conjeevaram Tālūkā and the two rivers bounding this *paṟṟu* are the Pālār and the rivulet which proceeds from the Tennēri lake; it is in this iraṇḍāṟṟu-paṟṟu that the Śrīvalimalai and the *nāḍu* named after it is also situated. Śrīvalimalai (a corruption of Śrīvallabhamalai) has to be identified with Palayaśivaram. Kaḷattūr-kōṭṭam is an ancient division of the Chōḷa period and receives its name from the village of Kaḷattūr, the railway station next to Chingleput. Udayambākkam, Kaḷattūr, Maṇappākkam and Puṇyappaṭṭu, which appears to be the same as Punnampaṭṭu, are in the Chingleput Taluka. Kshīranadi is the Saṅskṛit translation of the Tamiḷ name of the river Pālār. The temple of Virūpāksha mentioned in the grant is situated, as every one knows, in the Hampi-Hāḷupaṭṭaṇa, very near the river Tuṅgabhadrā.

TEXT [1].

FIRST PLATE FIRST SIDE.

१. श्रीगणाधिपतये नमः । नमस्तुंग[2]शिर(:)श्चुंबिचंद्र-

२. चामरचारवे । त्रैलो[क्य*]नगरारम्भमूलस्तंभाय [शं*] भवे । [।१*][3]हरेली[4]लावरा-

३. हस्य दंष्ट्रादंड: स पातु वः । हेमाद्रिकलशा यत्र धात्री छत्रश्रियं दधौ[।२*]

४. कल्याणायास्तु तधा[5]म प्रत्यूहतिमिरापहं[6] [।*]यद्गजोप्यगजोद्भूतं हरि-

५. णापि च पूज्यते । [।३*] अस्ति क्षीरमयादेवे[7]र्मथ्यमानान्महांबुधेः । नवनी-

६. तमिवोद्भूतमपनीततमो मह[:*]।[।४*] तस्याशीत[8]नयस्तपोभिरतुलैर[न्व]-

---

1. From inked impressions.
2. Anusvāra has been used in all places where Varga Pañchama is necessary.
3. Metre of verses 1-4 अनुष्टुभ्
4. Read हरेर्लीला
5. Read तद्धाम
6. In the end of words such as "तिमिरापहम्" Anusvāra is used instead of final ṁ.
7. Read द्दैवै
8. Read तस्यासीत्त

Second Inscription of Kṛishṇadēvarāya, No. V.

Ib

SCALE O. 7.

T. A. Gopinatha Rao. Half-Tone by Photo-Engraving Co., Madras.

७. र्थनामा बुधः पुण्यैरस्य पुरूरवा भुजबलैरायुर्द्विषां निघ्नतः । तस्य[।*]-

८. युर्ण[9]हुषोस्य तस्य परुषो युधे[10]ययाति[:*]क्षितौ ख्यातस्तस्य तु तुर्वसुर्वसुनि-

९. भःश्रीदेवयानीपतेः । [।५*][11]तद्वंशे देवकीजानिर्दिदीपे तिंमभूपतिः । यशश्वी[12]

१०. तुलुवेंद्रेषु यदोः कृष्ण इवान्वये । [।६*] ततोभूद्बुक्कमाजानी[13]रीश्वराक्षितिपा [ल]-

११. कः । अत्रासमगुणभ्रंशं मौलिरत्नं महीभुजां । [।७*] सरसादुदभूतस्मान[14][र]

१२. सावनिपालकः। देवकीनंदनात्कामो देवकीनंदनादिव । [।८*][15] विविधसुकृतोद्दा-

१३. मे रामेश्वरप्रमुखे मुहुर्मुदितहृदय[:*]स्थाने स्थाने [व्य][16]धत्त य-(य)थाविधिः[17] । बु-

१४. धपरिवृतो नानादानानि यो भुवि षोडश त्रिभुवनजनोद्गीतं [स्फी][तं*] यश[:*]

१५. पुनरुक्तय[न्*] (थाविधिः) [।।९*][18]कावेरीमासु[19] बध्वा बहळजलभरां यो विलं-

---

9. Read युर्नहुषो

10. Read युद्धे

11. Metre शार्दूलविक्रीडितम्

12. Read यशस्वी

13. Read जानि

14. Read तस्मान्न

15. Metre of verses 6-8 अनुष्टुभ्

16. Read व्यधत्त

17. Read विधि

18. Metre हरिणी

19. Read माशु

१६. ध्यैव शतृन्[20] जीवग्राहं गृहीत्वा समिति भुजबलातं[21] च राज्यं तदिय्यं[22] [।*]

१७. कृत्वा श्रीरंगपूर्वं तदपि निज[व*] शे पट्टणं यो बभाशे[23]कीत्ति[24]-स्तंभं निखातं[25]

१८. स्त्रिभुवनभुवन(:)स्तु[26]यमानापदानः । [।१०*][27]चेरं चोळं च पांड्यं तदपि च मधु-

१९. रावल्लभं मानभूषं वीर्योदग्रं तुरुष्कं गजपतिनृपतिं चापि जि-

२०. त्वा तदंन्यान्[28] । आगंगातीरलं[का*]प्रथमचरमभूभृत[29]टांतं नितांतं ख्या-

२१. त[:*] क्षोणीपतीनां स्त्रजमिव सिरसा[30] शासनं यो व्यतानीन्[31] । [।११*] तिप्पाजीनाग-

२२. लादेव्यो कं[32]सल्याश्रीसुमित्रयोः । देव्योरिव नृसिंहेंद्रा[33]तस्मात्पंक्तिर-

२३. [था]वि[34]व । [।१२*][35] वीरौ विनदनौ[36] रामलक्ष्मणाविव नंदनौ [।*] जातौ [वीरौ][37]नृसिं-

20. Read शत्रून्
21. Read बलात्तं
22. Read तदीयम्
23. Read बभासे
24. Read कीर्ति
25. Read निखाय
26. Read त्रिभुवनभवनस्तू
27. Metre of verses 10-11 स्रग्धरा
28. Read तदन्यान्
29. Read त्तटांतं
30. Read शिरसां
31. Read व्यतानीत्
32 Read देव्योः कौसल्या
33. Read त्तस्मा
34. Read थादिव
35. Metre of verses 12-13 अनुष्टुभ्
36. Read विनयिनौ
37. Read वीर

२४. हेद्र[38]कृष्णरायमहीपती । [।१३*] वीरश्रीनारसिंह्म:[39]स विजय-
नगरे रत्न-

२५. सिंह्मा[40]सनस्थ: कीर्त्या नीत्या निरस्यं[41]नृगनळनहुषानप्य-
वन्यां व-

२६. दांन्या[42] । आ [से*]तोरासुमेरोरवनिसुरनुतस्वै[43]रमाचोदया-
द्रेरापाश्वां[44]त्या-

२७. चलांतादखिलहृदयमावर्ज्य राज्यं सशास[45] । [।१४*] [46]नाना
दानान्यकाषीत्क-[47]

२८. नकसदसि यः श्रीविरूपाक्षदेवस्थाने श्रीकाळहस्तीशितुरपि न-

२९. गरे वेङ्कट्टाद्रौ[48]च कांच्यां । श्रीशैले शोणशैले महति हरिहरे हो-
[ब]ले

३०. संगमे च श्रीरंगे कुंभघोणे हततमशि[49] महानंदितीर्थे निवृत्तौ ।
[।१५*]

३१. गोकर्णे रामशेतौ[50]जगति तदितरेष्वप्यशेषेषु पुंण्य[51]स्थानेष्वा-

FIRST PLATE SECOND SIDE.

३२. रब्धनानाविधबहळमहादानवारिप्रवाहैः । यस्यो-

---

38. Read हेन्द्र
39. Read सिंह
40. Read सिंहा
41. Read स्यन्नृग
42. Read दान्वान्
43. Read स्वैर
44. Read पाश्चात्या
45 Read शशास
46. Metre of verses 14-17 स्रग्धरा
47. Read कार्षी
48. Read वेङ्कटाद्रौ
49. Read तमसि
50. Read सेतौ
51. Read पुण्य

३३. दंचत्तुरंगप्रकरखुररजःसु[52]ष्यदंभोधि[म]ग्न(:) क्ष्माभृ [त्प]-

३४. क्षच्छिदोद[53]त्तरकुलिशधरोत्कंठिता कुंठिताभूत् । [१६*]
ब्रह्मांडं

३५. वि[श्व] चक्रं [घ*]टमुदितमहाभूतकं रत्नधेनुः[54]शप्तांभोधीं[श्च]
कल्प-

३६. क्षितिरुहलतिके कांचनीं कामधेनुं । स्वर्णक्ष्मा यो[55] हिरं-[56]

३७. ण्याश्वरथमपि तुलापूरुषं गोसहस्रं हेमाश्वं हेमगर्भं कन-

३८. ककरिरथं पंचलांगल्यतानीत् । [।१७*] प्राज्यं प्रसाश्य[57]
निर्विघ्नं रा-

३९. [ज्यं]द्यामिव शाशितुं[58] । तस्मिन् [गु]णेन विख्याते क्षिते-
रिंद्रे दिवं ग-

४०. ते । [।१८*][59]ततोप्यवार्य्यवीर्यश्रीकृष्णरायमहीपतिः । बि-
भर्त्ति[60]मणिके-

४१. [यू]रनिर्विशेषं महीं भुजे । [१९.*] कीर्त्या यश्य[61] समंततः
प्रस्तुतया[62] वि-

४२. श्वं रुचैक्यं व्रजेदित्याशंक्य पुरा पुरारिरभस[63]भ्दालेक्षणः प्रा-

---

52. Read जश्शुष्य
53. Read यत्तर
54. Read धेनुं
55. Read स्वर्णक्ष्मां
56. Read हिर
57. Read प्रशास्य
58. Read शासितुम्
59. Metre of verses 18-19 अनुष्टुभ्
60. Read बिभर्त्ति
61. Read कीर्त्या यस्य
62. Read प्रसृतया
63. Read रभवद्भा

Second Inscription of Kṛishṇadēvarāya, No. V.

IIa

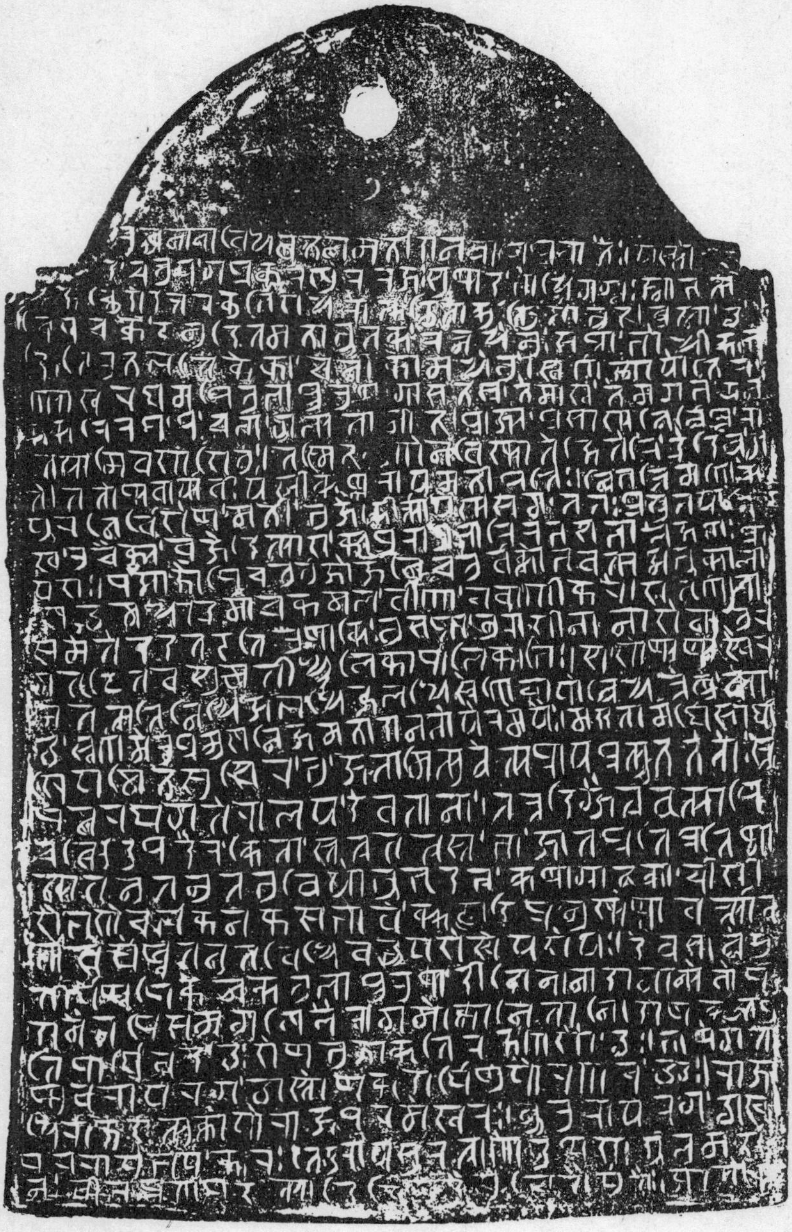

1 32 33 34 35 36 37 38 39 40 41 42 43 44 45 46 47 48 49 50 51 52 53 54 55 56 57 58 59 60

SCALE O. 7.

T. A. GOPINATHA RAO.

Half-Tone by Photo-Engraving Co., Madras.

४३. यशः । पद्माक्षोपि चतुर्भुजोजनि चतुर्वक्त्रोभवत्पद्मभू[:*]
काली

४४. खड्गमधाद्रमा च कमलं वीणां च वाणी करे । [64][।२०*]शतृ-
णा[65] वा-

४५. समेते ददत इति रुषा किंनु स[प्तां]बुराशीनाना[66]शेना[67]तु[रं]-

४६. गतृटित[68]वसुमतीधूळिकापालिकाभिः । संशोष्य (ष्य) स्वैर-

४७. [मे]त[त्प्र]तिनिधिजलधि(जलधि)[श्रे]णिकां यो विधत्ते ब्र[ह्मां]-

४८, डं*स्वर्णमेरुप्रमुखनिजमहादानतोयैरमेयैः। [।२१*][69] मद्दताम-
र्थिसार्था[70]

४९. श्रियमिह सुचिरं भुंजतामित्युवेत्य[71]प्रायः प्रत्यूहहेतो(:)स्त-

५०. पनरय†गतेरालयं देवतानां । तत्तदिग्जैत्रवृत्या[72]पि

५१. च बिरुदुपदैरंकितांस्तत्र तत्र स्तंभां जात[73] प्रति(प्रति)ष्ठा-[74]

५२. न्यतनुत (नुत)भुवि यो भूभृदभ्रंकषाग्रान्। [।२२*] कांचीश्री-

५३. शैलशो[णा*]चलकनकसभावेंकटा[75]द्रिप्रमुख्येष्वावर्त्याव-

५४. र्त्य [स]र्वेष्वतनुत विधिवद्भूयशे स्नेयशे[76]यः। देव[स्था]ने[षु]

---

64. Metre शार्दूलविक्रीडितम्
65. Read शत्रूणां
66. Read न्नाना
67. Read सेना
68. Read त्रुटित
*. Read ड
69. Metre of verses 21-23 स्रग्धरा
70. Read मद्दत्तामर्थिसार्था
71. Read त्यवेत्य
† Read रथ
72. Read तत्तद्दिग्जैत्रवृत्त्या
73. Read स्तम्भाञ्जात
74. Read प्रतिष्ठा
75. Read वेङ्कटा
76. Read भूयसे श्रेयसे

५५. तीर्थेष्वपि कनकतुलापूरुषादीनि नानादानान्येतो[77]प-

५६. दानै[र]पि सममखिलैरागमोक्तानि तानि। [२३*] दोषक्क[तप्र]-

५७. तिप्रार्थिवदंड: शेषभुजाक्कतिरक्षणशौंड: । भाषेगेत-

५८. प्पुवरायरगंडा[78]स्तोषक्कदर्थिषु यो रणचंडड:[79] । [।२४*][80] राजा-

५९. धिराजइत्युक्तो यो राजपरमेश्वर: । मूरुरायरगंडा[81]श्च

६०. पररायभयंकर: [।।२५*][82] हिंदुरायसुरत्राणो दुष[83]शार्दूल-मर्द-

६१. न: [।*] वीरप्रताप इत्यादि ०० दै[84]रुचितैर्युतै:[85]। [।२६*] आ[लोक]-

SECOND PLATE: FIRST SIDE.

६२. य महाराय जय जीवेदि[86] वादिभि: । अंगवं[ग*]कालिंगा-

६३. दै राजभि: शेव्यते[87] च य: । [।२७*] स्तुत्यौदार्य[:*] सुधीभि: स विजय-

६४. नगरे रत्नसिंहास[न*]स्थ: क्ष्मापालान् कृष्णरायक्षितिप-

६५. तिरधरीकृत्य नीत्या नृगादीन् । आपूर्वाद्रेरथास्ताक्षिति-

---

77. Read न्येवो

78. Read गण्ड

79. Read चण्ड:

80. Metre दोधक

81. Read गण्डश्च

82. Metre of verses 25-27 अनुष्टुभ

83. Read दुष्ट

84. Read बिरुदै

85. Read र्युत:

86. Read जीवेति

87 Read सेव्यते

Second Inscription of Kṛishṇadēvarāya, No. V.

IIb

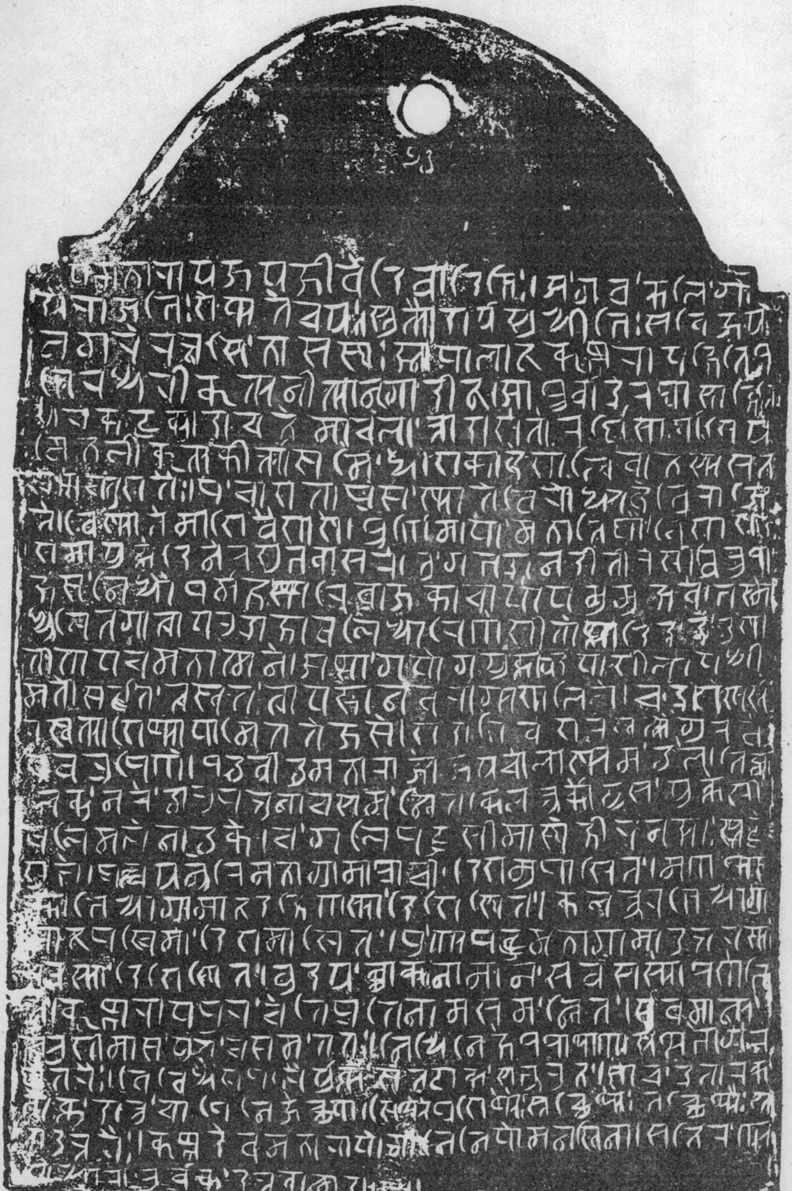

SCALE O. 7.

GOPINATHA RAO. Half-Tone by Photo-Engraving Co., Madras

६६. धरकट्टका[88]दा च हेमाचलांत्ता[89]दा[से]तोरर्थिसार्थ(।)श्रिय-

६७. मिह [बह*]लीकृत्य कीर्त्या समिंधे । [।२८*][90]शकाब्दे शालिवाहस्य सह-

६८. स्त्रेण चतु[:*] शतैः । पंचाशता प्रसंख्याते विरोध्यब्दे [वि]राजि-

६९. ते । [।२९*][91] विख्याते माशि[92] वैशाखे (।) पूर्णिमायां महातिथौ । विशाख०[93]-

७०. समायुक्ते दिनेर[94]शुभवासरे । [।३०] तुंगभद्रानदीती [रे] श्री-विरूपा-

७१. क्षसंनिधौ [।*] पर्महस[95] [प] रिव्राजकाचार्याय मुमुक्षवे । [।३१*] भस्म [ो*]-

७२. द्धूलितगात्राय रुद्राक्षावलिधारिणे [।*] शीतोष्णादिद्वंद्व[96]दुखा-

७३. तीताय च महात्मने । [।३२*] अष्टांगयोगयुक्ताय दयाशी-लाय[धी]-

७४. मते । सर्वतन्त्रस्वतन्त्राय [जा] नव[97]राग्यशालिने । [।३३*] चंद्र[शेखर] स-

७५. रस्वत्या शि[98]ष्यायामिततेजसे* । सदाशिव[स]रस्वत्यै गुरवे

---

88. Read कटका
89. Read चलान्ता
90. Metre स्रग्धरा
91. Metre of verses 29-42½ अनुष्टुभ्
92. Read मासि
93. Read विशाखर्क्ष
94. Metre दिनेश
95. Read परहंस
96. Read द्वन्द्व
97. Read ज्ञानवैराग्य
98. Read स्वत्याश्शिष्या

* एकमक्षरमधिकं दृश्यते

७६. शिवरूपिणे । [।३४*] पडवीडुमहाराज्ये जयचोळाख्यमंडले । तिक्कों-

७७. ळिकं नूरेंडारुपत्तुना च समंन्विते[99]। [।३५*] कळत्तूर्कोट्टसं-युक्ते श्री-

७८. वलिमलेनाडुके [।*] चंगलिपट्टुसीमास्थे क्षीरनद्या(:)स्तटे

७९. शुभे । [।३६*] प्रळ्ळयनूरिमहाग्रामा[100]प्राचीं दिशमुपाश्रितं [।*] मणप्पा-

८०. क्काभिधाग्रामात्[101]दक्षिणस्यां दिशि स्थितं । [।३७*]कळत्तू-रभिधाग्रा-[102]

८१. [मा]त् पश्चिमां दिशमाश्रितं । पुंण्यपट्टुमहाग्रामादुत्तरस्यां

८२. (त्तरस्यां) दिशि स्थितं । [।३८*] वुदयंब्बाक्कनामानं सर्व-सस्योपशोभि-

८३. तं । कृष्णरायपुरं चेति प्रतिनामसमंन्वितं[103]। [।३९*] सव-मान्यं[104]

८४. चतुशीमा[105]संयुतं च समंततः । निधिनिक्षेपपाषाणाद्यष्टभोगैर-

८५. थेतरैः । [।४०*] विविधै[र्*]सफलैर्युक्तं सतटाकं सभूरुहं । आचन्द्रतारकं

८६. भोक्तं दात्तुं[106]चापि निजेच्छया ।[।४१*] सिष्यै प्रशिष्यैः[107] स्तच्छिष्यैः तच्छिष्यैः स्त-[108]

---

99. Read समन्विते
100. Read ग्रामात्प्राची
101. Read भिधग्रामाद्
102. Read भिधग्रामात्
103. Read समन्वितम्
104. Read सर्वमान्यं
105. Read चतुस्सीमा
106. Read भोक्तुं दातुं
107. Read शिष्यैः प्रशिष्यै
108. Read तच्छिष्यैस्त

Second Inscription of Kṛishṇadēvarāya, No. V.

IIIa

SCALE O. 7.

८७. त्तदुत्तैरः । कृष्णदेवमहारायो मानिनियो मनश्विना[109]। [।४२*]
सहिरंण्य[110]

८८. [प*]योधारापूर्वकं दत्तवान् मुदा । ॥

८९. तदिदमवनीवानिपक[111]विनुतधरा यश्य[112] कृष्णरायश्य[113] शास-

९०. नमुरुकविवैभवनिवहनिदानस्य भूरिदानस्य । [।४३½][114]
कृष्णदेवम-

९१. हारायशासन्देन सभ[।*]पतिः । अभाणीन् मृदुसंदर्भ तदिदं
तांम्र-[115]

९२. शासनं । [।४४½*][116] कृष्णदेवमहारायशासनं मल्लणात्मजः।
[त्व]ष्टा श्रीवीरणाचा-

९३. र्यो व्यलिखं तांम्रशासनः। [४५½*]दानपालनयोर्मध्ये दानाच्छ्रे-
योनुपालनं दा-

९४. नात्स्वर्गमवाप्नोति पालानादच्युत [117]पदं। [।४६½*]स्वदत्ता-
द्विगुणं पुण्यं परदत्तानुपा-

९५. लनं परदत्तापहारेण स्वदत्तं नि[ष्फ]लं भवेत्। [।४७½*]
स्वदत्ता परदत्ता [118] वा यो हरे-

---

109. Read माननीयो मनस्विनाम्

110. Read सहिरण्य

111. Read वनीपक

112. Read यस्य

113. Read कृष्णरायस्य ।

114. Metre गीत्यार्या

115. Read ताम्र

116. Metre of verses 44½-49½ अनुष्टुभ्

117. Read दच्युतं पदं

118. Read दत्तां परदत्तां

९६. ति वसुंधरात्[119] । षष्टिर्वरुष[120]सहस्राणि विष्टायां[121] जायते क्रिमि[:*] । [।४८½*] एकैव भगि-

९७. नी लोके सर्वेषामेव भूभुजां । न भोज्या न करग्राह्या विप्रदत्ता वसुंध-

९८. रा । [।४९½*] सामान्योयं [122] धर्मशेतुं[123]नृपाणां काले काले पालनीयो भवद्भिः ।

९९. सर्वानेतान् भाविनः पार्थिवेन्द्रान् भूयो भूयो याचते राम-चन्द्रः ॥ [५०½*][124]

१००. श्रीविरूपक्ष[125] ॥

(ABSTRACT OF THE CONTENTS.)

(The historical part of this inscription is similaı to that in No. IV above).

On a Sunday which corresponded with the full moon tithi of the month Vaiśākha in the year Virōdhin, S' 1450 and the nakshatra Viśākha, the king Kṛishṇadēvarāya granted the village of Udayambākkam under the name of Kṛishṇarāya-puram, in the presence of the god Virūpāksha, on

---

119. Read हरेत वसुन्धराम्

120. Read षष्टिं वर्ष

121. Read विष्ठायां

122. Read सामान्योऽयं

123. Read सेतुर्नृपाणां

124. Metre शालिनी

125. Read विरूपाक्ष

the bank of the river Tuṅgabhadrā to Sadāśiva-Sarasvati, the disciple of Chandraśēkhara Sarasvati.

The village granted was situated in the Cheṅgalipaṭṭu Śimā, a portion of the Śrīvalimalai-nāḍu, situated in the Kaḷattūr-kōṭṭam, a division of the Tirukkāḷigaṉraṇḍāṟṟu-ppaṟṟu, in the Paḍavī-ḍurājya which was a sub-division of the Jayachōḷa-maṇḍalam.

This village was situated on the east of the great *agrahāra* named Praḷḷayanūr, on the south of the village of Maṇappākkam, on the west of the village of Kaḷattūr and on the north of the great village of Puṇyappaṭṭu.

The document was composed by Sabhāpati and was engraved on copper-plates by Vīraṇāśāri, the son of Mallaṇa.

No. VI.

A FRAGMENTARY INSCRIPTION OF VIJAYANAGARA KINGS OF THE KARNĀṬA OR THE LAST DYNASTY.

THIS fragmentary inscription is engraved on only one side of a plate, which belonged to a set, the remaining plates of which seem to have been lost. It is written in the Nandināgari characters and in the Sanskṛit language. In it the genealogy of the kings of the Karnāṭa dynasty is traced from the moon. Some of the descendants of the moon who were the ancestors of these kings are said to be Budha, Purūravas, Āyus, Nahusha, Yayāti, Pūru, Bharata, Śantanu ; the fourth from this last was Vijaya ; from him was born Abhimanyu and from him Parīkshit. The eighth in descent from Parīkshit was Nanda ; the ninth from this king was Chaḷikka ; the seventh from Chaḷikka was Rājanarēndra ; and the tenth in descent from him was Bijjaḷēndra, whose third descendant was Vīra

Hemmāḷiraya, the lord of Māyāpuri. The fourth from him came Tāta Pinnama, the first real ancestor of this dynasty. From here the genealogy as far as it goes in this fragment is as follows :—

Tāta-Pinnama I
|
Sōmidēva
|
Rāghavadēva
|
Pinnama II
(the lord of Āravīṭinagara)
|
Bukka.

The subsequent genealogy of this family as we meet with in other copper-plate grants is given for the information of the readers of this brochure (1).

(1). Taken from Epigraphia Indica, Volume III page 238.

- 5. Bukka, md. Ballāmbikā.
  - 6. Rāma I, md. Lakkāmbikā.
    - 7. Raṅga I, md. Tirumalāmbikā.
      - 8. Rāma II (also known as Aliya Rāmarāya) md. Sister of Sadāśiva (A. D. 1565).
        - 18. Raṅga IV (one of five brothers)
          - 19. Peda-Vēṅkata II md. Baṅgārama. (S' 1556-1558)
          - 20. Pina-Vēṅkata or China Vēṅkata
            - 23. Raṅga VI. adopted by Gōpāla (S' 1566)
      - 9. Tirumala I md. Vēṅgalāmbikā
        - 11. Raghunātha.
        - 12. Raṅga. II. (S' 1497-1506)
        - 13. Rāma III.
        - 14. Vēṅkata I. md. 1. Vēṅgalāmbā 2. Rāghavāmbā 3. Pedōbamāmbā 4. Krishṇamāmbā 5. Koṇḍamāmbā
          - 15. Tirumala II.
          - 16. Raṅga III
            - 17. Rāma IV (one of several brothers.)
      - 10. Vēṅkatādri. (A.D. 1565)
        - 21. Raṅga V
          - 22. Gōpāla adopted Raṅga VI

From this incomplete document it is impossible to say to whose reign it belonged.

TEXT [1].

१. श्रीवेंकटेशाय नमः । [।*] यस्य संपर्कपुण्ये-

२. न नारीरत्नमभूच्छिला । यदुपास्यं सुमनसां

३. तद्वस्तुद्वंद्वमाश्रये । [।१*] यस्य द्विरदवक्त्राद्याः पारिषद्या[2]

४. परश्शतं । विघ्नं निघ्नंति भजतां विष्वक्सेनं तमा-

५. श्रये । [।२*] जयति क्षीरजलधेर्जातं सव्येक्षणं हरेः । आ-

६. लंबनं चकोराणाममरायुष्करं महः । [।३*][3]पौत्रस्तस्य

७. पुरूरवा बुधसुतस्तस्यायुरस्यात्मजः (।) संजज्ञे न-

८. हुषा[4]ययातिरभवस्तस्माच्च पुरु[5]स्ततः । तद्वंशे भर-

९. तो बभूव नपति[6]स्तत्संततौ शंतनुः (।) तत्तुर्‍यो विज-

१०. याभि[7]मन्युरुदभू[8]स्तस्मात्परीक्षिस्तत[9]ः। [।४*][10]नंदस्तस्या-

११. ष्टमोभूत्समजनि नवमस्तस्य राज्ञश्चक्कि[11]क्ष्माप[स्त]-

१२. [स्स][12]त्तमश्रीपातिरुचिरभवद्राजपूर्वो नरेन्द्रः । त[स्या]-

१३. सीद्बि[13]ज्जळेन्द्रो दशम यिह[14] नृपो वीरहेंमाळिरा-

१४. यस्तार्तीयीको मुरारौ कृतनतिरुदभूस्तस्य[15] माय[ा]-

१५. पुरीशः । [।५*][16]तत्तुर्योजनि तातपिन्नममहीपा[लो] नि-

---

1. From inked impressions.
2. Read पारिषद्याः
3. Metre of verses 1—3 अनुष्टुभ्
4. Read हुषो
5. Read त्तस्माच्च पूरु
6. Read नृपति
7. Read योऽभिमन्यु
8. Read त्तस्मा
9. Read त्ततः
10. Metre शार्दूलविक्रीडितम्
11. Read श्चलिक्क
12. Read त्सत्तम
13. Read द्विज्जळेन्द्रो
14. Read इह
15. Read त्तस्य
16. Metre स्रग्धरा

१६. [जा]लोकनात्रस्तात्रिग[17]स्ततोजनि हरन[18]दुर्गाणि स-

१७. [प्तो][19]हितात् । अन्हैकेन[20] स सोमिदेवनृपतिस्तसौव[21] जज्ञे सु-

१८. तो (।) वीरो राघवदेवराडिति तश्रीपिंनमोभूनृप[22]: । [।६*] [23] आर-

१९. वीटिनगरीविभोरभूतस्य[24] बुक्कधरणीपतिस्सुतः । येन

२०. साळुवनृसिंहराज्यमप्येधमानमहसा स्थिरीकृतः[25] । [।७*][26]

२१. [स्वः]कामिनीं स्वतनुकान्तिभिराक्षिपंतीं बुक्कावनीपति-

२२. [लको] बुधकल्पशाखी । कल्याणिनीं कमलनाभ यिवाब्धि- कन्य[।][27]

TRANSLATION.

(Verse 1). I take refuge in that pair of objects which is to be worshipped by the gods, (and) at whose meritorious touch a stone became the best of woman.

---

17. Read लोकनत्रस्तामित्रगण
18. Read हरन्दुर्गाणि
19. Read साहितात्
20. Read अहैकेन
21. Read तस्यैव
22. Read ततःश्रीपिंनमोऽभूनृपः
23. Metre शार्दूलविक्रीडितम्
24. Read तस्य
25. Read स्थिरीकृतम्
26. Metre रथोद्धता
27. Read इवाब्धिकन्यां

(Verse 2). I take refuge in that Vishvaksēna whose more than hundred attendants, the elephant-headed (Gaṇēśa) etc., remove the obstacles (in the way) of (his) devotees.

(Verse 3). Victorious is the luminary (*viz.*, the Moon) which rose from the milk-sea (which is) the left eye of Hari (Vishṇu), (which is) the support of the *chakōra* (birds), (and) which sustains the life of the gods.

(Verse 4). The grandson of him (*viz.*, the Moon) (was) Budha's son Purūravas; his (son was) Āyus; his son was Nahusha; from him was born Yayāti; (and) from him Pūru. In his race was born king Bharata; in his lineage Śantanu; the fourth from him was Vijaya; from him was born Abhimanyu; (and) from him Parīkshit.

(Verse 5). The eighth (in descent) from him was Nanda; the ninth from this king was king Chaḷikka; the seventh from him was Narēndra (whose name was) preceded by Rāja (*i.e.*, Rāja-narēndra), (and) who was devoted to Śrīpati (Vishṇu); the tenth from him in this (world) was king Bijjaḷēndra; (and) the third from him was Vīra-Hemmāḷirāya, the lord of Māyāpuri, who prostrated himself before Murārī (Vishṇu).

(Verse 6). The fourth from him was king Tāta-Pinnama, at whose sight the crowd of

Fragmentary Inscription of the Karnāṭa Dynasty, No. VI.

SCALE O. 7.

T. A. GOPINATHA RAO. Half-Tone by Photo-Engraving Co., Madras.

No. VII.

AN INSCRIPTION OF THE TIME OF VIJAYA RAGHUNĀTHA TOṆḌAIMĀN OF PUDUKKOTTAI; ŚAKA SAMVAT, 1613.

THIS is an inscription which is engraved on the two sides of a single plate, in Tamiḻ characters and alphabet. The rectangular plate has a small circular top, on the front portion of which are cut the figures of a Liṅga and of a Dēvī, each separated by lines which represent canopies over their head; on the back of this circular portion of the plate are cut the words *Śri Rāmajayam* in Telugu characters. The Kumbhakōṇam *maṭha* is intimately connected with Jambukēśvaram in the island of Śrīraṅgam and hence, I am inclined to take the Liṅga and the Dēvī to be meant by the engraver to refer to Jambunātha and His consort Akhilaṇḍēśvarī. The writing on the plate is in good condition, but the plate itself is broken in its corners and the damage to the inscription incurred thereby is however practically nothing.

The record belongs to the time of the Pudukkōṭṭai chief Vijaya Raghunātha Toṇḍaimān, son of Tirumalaiyappa Toṇḍaimān and is dated the 15th day of the month Tai in the year Dundubhi, which was also the Śaka year 1613. In this year, the servants of Vijaya Raghunātha Toṇḍaimān, who held lands in the southern division of Anbil, made a gift in perpetuity of certain paddy and money payments to one Veṅkaṭakṛishṇayyan, son of Veṅkaṭayyan of Kāñchīpuram. The inscription begins with a verbose and bombastic panegyric like those of the kings of Vijayanagara Empire, which they themselves did not claim but which has been usually employed by the Ramnad Zamindars in their copper-plate grants. As is also usual with these latter grants, all the kings of the Vijayanagara Empire are enumerated one after another in an irregular, unchronological order. The donee, Venkaṭakṛishṇayyan of Kāñchīpuram, seems to be an agent of the *maṭha* sent to be in charge of the landed estates belonging to the *maṭha*, which were situated in the Trichinopoly District and adjoining Jambukēśvaram. Anbil, Tiruvāśi and the adjacent places have even now respectable families of Kaḷḷars, who bear the title *nāḍāvān* (a corrupt form of *nāḍāḻvān*); perhaps the ancestors of these were holding *jaghirs* under the Pudukkōṭṭai chieftain enemies trembled; from him was born that king Śōmidēva who took from the enemy seven forts in a single day; his heroic son was king Rāghavadēva; (and) from him was born the glorious king Pinnama.

(Verse 7). The son of this lord of the city of Āravīṭi was king Bukka, whose power was (continually) rising, (and) who firmly established even the kingdom of Sāḷuva-Nṛisiṁha.

(Verse 8). Just as Vishṇu (married) Lakshmī, Bukka, the ornament of kings (and) the *kalpa*-tree, to scholars, married the prosperous Ballāmbikā, who surpassed the celestial nymphs by her personal beauty, (and) whose virtue was highly respected.

Inscription of the reign of Vijaya Raghunātha Toṇḍaimān of Pudukkōṭṭai, Śaka Samvat, 1613, No. VII.

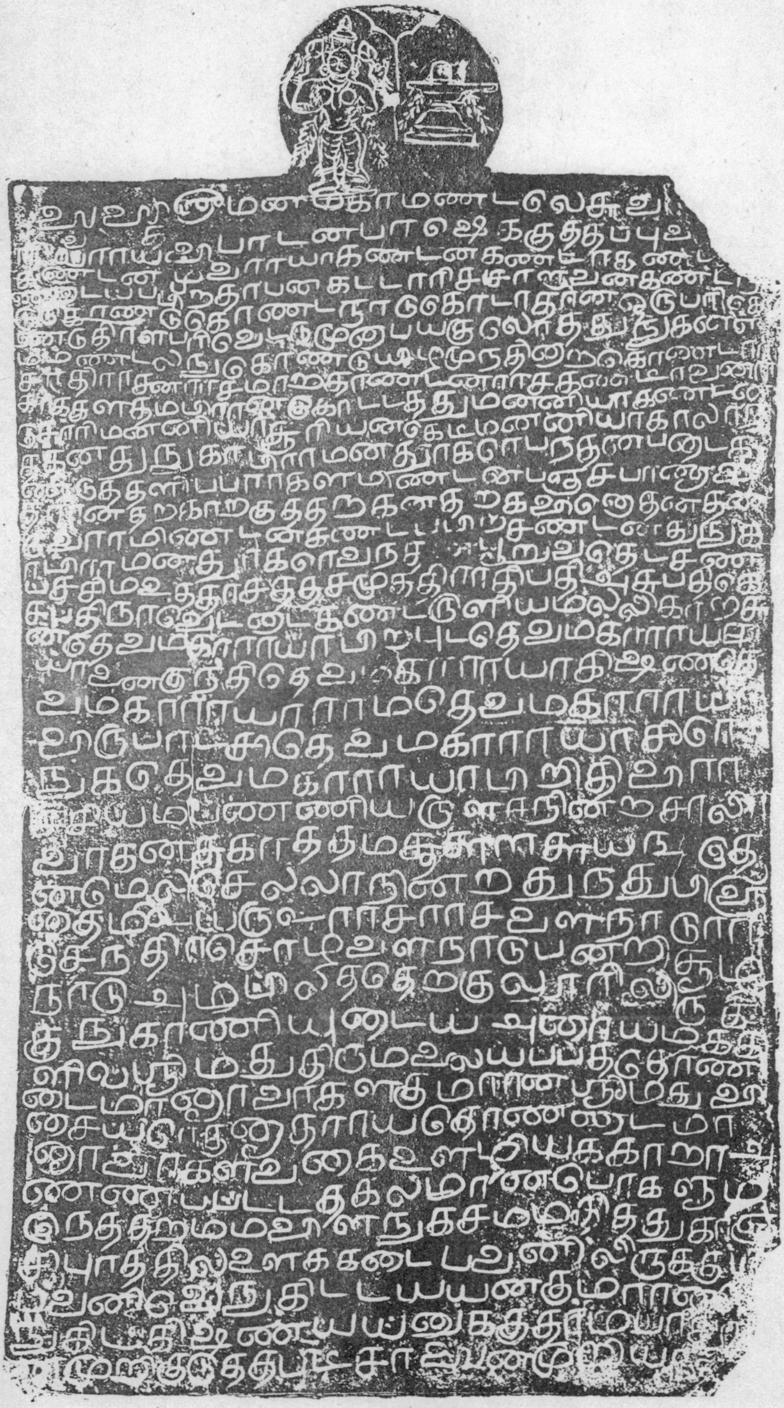

SCALE O. 7.

T. A. Gopinatha Rao. Half-Tone By Photo-Engraving Co., Madras.

and rendered military service to him. The actual grants made by these to the brāhmaṇa agent of the *maṭha* are:—

(*a*) a *kuṟuṇi* of paddy per head per mensem to be paid by all those who held appointments (?) under the Toṇḍaimān;

(*b*) a sum equal to the pay of one man to be paid as *umbaḷam* by every ten of the servant classes of men;

(*c*) they should also give eight *marakkāls* of paddy per annum;

(*d*) three *paḍis* of rice per diem for the Paḷḷaya-chchōttu-kaṭṭaḷai; and lastly

(*e*) two pairs of male cloths and two female cloths per annum also had to be given as long as the moon and the sun lasted.

The village of Anbil is said to have been situated in the Panṟi-śūḷ-nāḍu of the Rājēndra-śōḷanāḍu, a sub-division of the Rājarājavaḷanāḍu. This village is situated on the north bank of the river Koleroon.

The Vijayanagara Emperors who are mentioned in the document are given in the following order: Mallikārjunadēva Mahārāya, Prauḍhadēva Mahārāya, Yānaigundi Dēva Mahārāya, Virūpākshadēva Mahārāya and Śrīraṅgadēva Mahārāya. The Vijayanagara (or rather the Chandragiri) prince who might be taken to be the contemporary of the Pudukkōṭṭai chieftain Vijaya Raghunātha Toṇḍaimān is either Raṅga VI or his successor.

First Side.

1. ஸ்வஸ்தி ஸ்ரீமன் மகாமண்டலேசுவ[ரன் அ]-
2. ரியராயவிபாடன் பாஷெக்குத்தப்புவ[ராயர]
3. கண்டன் மூவராயரகண்டன் கண்டரகண்ட[ன்]...
4. ண்டைப் பிரதாபன் கட்டாரிச்சாளுவன் கண்ட ந[ா]-
5. டு கொண்டு கொண்டநாடு கொடாதான் ஒரு பரி கெ[ா]-
6. ண்டு திரள் பரிவெட்டுமுடைய குலோத்துங்கன் எ-
7. ம் மண்டலங்கொண்டு யீழமுந்திறை கொண்டரா-
8. சாதி ராசன் ராச மாற்தாண்டன் ராச கண்டீரவன் ரா-
9. சாக்கள் தம்பிரான் கோட்டத்து மன்னியர் கண்டன்
10. சொரிமன்னியர் சூரியன் கெடிமன்னியர் காலாந்-
11. தகன் துங்காபிராமன் துர்கரேபந்தன் படைக-
12. ண்டுத்தளிப்பார்கள் மிண்டன் பஞ்சபாண [வ]-
13. தாரன் தற்க(ா)ற்குத்தற்கன் தற்கவிநோதன் தண்-
14. டுவார் மிண்டன் சண்டப்பிறசண்டன் துங்க-
15. ாபிராமன் துர்கரேவந்தன்பூறுவ தெட்சண
16. பச்சிம உத்தர சத்த சமுத்திராதிபதி அசுபதி கெ-

Inscription of the reign of Vijaya Raghunātha Tondaimān, No. VII.

SCALE O. 7.

GOPINATHA RAO.

Half-Tone By Photo-Engraving Co., Madras.

17. சபதி நாவேட்டை கண்டருளிய மல்லிகாற்ச-
18. னதேவமகாராயர் பிறபுடதேவ மகாராயர்
19. யானைகுந்தி தேவமகாராயர் கிஷ்ணதே-
20. வமகாராயர் ராமதேவ மகாராயர்
21. விருபாட்சி தேவமகாராயர் சீரெ-
22. ங்க தேவமகாராயர் பிறிதிவி ரா-
23. ச்சியம் பண்ணியருளாநின்ற சாலி-
24. வாகன சகாத்தம் ௲௭௱௪ இத-
25. ன்மேல் செல்லாநின்ற துந்துபிவரு
26. ஷ தைமீ ௰௯உ ராசராசவளநாடு ரா-
27. சேந்திரசோழவளநாடு பன்றிசூழ்
28. நாடு அம்பில்தெற்குவூரி லிருக்-
29. குங்காணியுடைய அரைய மக்க-
30. ளில் ஸ்ரீமது திருமலையப்பத் தொண்-
31. டைமானுரவர்கள் குமாரன் ஸ்ரீமது வி-
32. சைய ரெகுனாதராய தொண்டைமா-
33. னுரவர்கள் வகை ஊழியக்காறர் அ-
34. ண்ணப்பட்ட தகலமான பேர்களும்
35. இந்த தற்மம் விளங்கச் சம்மதித்து காஞ்-
36. சி புரத்தில் உள்க்கடை பவனிலிருக்கும்
37. பவனி வெங்கிட்டய்யன் குமாரன் [வெ]-
38. ங்கிட கிஷ்ணய்யனுக்கு தாம்பரசா[ஸ]-
39. ன முறிகுடுத்தபடி சாஸன முறியாவ[து]

Second Side.

ஸ்ரீராமஜெயம்.

40. ...ப படிவாங்கிற பேர்கள் சகல-
41. [பேர்]க்கும் சனம் க-க்கு மாதம் ஒண்ணு-

42. க்கு நெல்லுக்குறுணி[யும்] சீவிதம்
43. பத்திஇருக்குற ஊழியக்காறர் ச-
44. கலருக்கும் பத்து ஆள் சீவிதத்-
45. துக்கு ஒருஆள் சீவிதம் உம்ப-
46. ளம் போக மத்தஆள் ஒன்றுக்கு
47. வருஷாவதி எட்டுமெரக்கா நெல்-
48. லும் பள்ளையச்சொத்து கட்டளை
49. அரிசி தினம் மூணுபடியும் வருஷ-
50. ாவதி ரெண்டு சோடு சோமனும் ரெ-
51. ண்டுசேலையும் குடுக்ககடவோமாக-
52. வும் இந்த தற்மம் இந்தப்பிறகாரம் ச-
53. ந்திராதி சூரியாதித்த வரைக்கும் வாங்கி-
54. கொண்டு சுகத்திலே யிருக்க கடவேனாக-
55. வும் இந்த தற்மத்துக்கு யாதா மொருத்த-
56. ன் தடை பண்ணினாலும் பக்குவம் பண்-
57. ணினாலும் காசியிலே கெங்கை கரை-
58. யிலே காராம்பசுவை கொண்ணவன்
59. பிறம்மத்தியை ஸ்ரீகத்தியை பண்ணி-
60. னவன் எந்த தோஷத்தில் நரகத்தில் அ-
61. னுபவிப்பானோ அந்த தோஷம் அ-
62. னுபவிப்பானாகவும் இந்ததற்மம் ஊழி-
63. யக்காறர் அண்ணப்பட்ட சகலமான
64. பேர்களுக்கும் சரி இந்ததற்மம் யாதாமொ-
65. ருத்தர் விளங்க நடப்பிக்குராகளோ அ-
66. வர்களுக்கு ஆயிரத்தெட்டு சிவாலியம்
67. அக்கிறகார சத்திரங்கள் பண்ணின ப-
68. லன்னுண்டாய் செரிஞ்சீவியாய் புத்தி-

69. ர பவுத்திராதி சம்பத்தோடே யிரு-
70. [ப்]பார்கள் இந்தபடி எழிதினது பெரி-
71. ...ாசாரியர் குமாரன் வேலாயுதம் கை[ய்]-
72. [யெழுத்]து பெரியஞயகி அம்மன் துணை.

ABSTRACT OF CONTENTS.

(First Side). Be it well! Mallikārjunadēvamahārāyar — Prauḍhadēvamahārāyar — Kṛishṇadēvamahārāyar of Ānēgundi—Rāmadēvamahārāyar — Virūpākshadēvamahārāyar—Śrīraṅgadēvamahārāyar,—who bore the titles *Mahāmanḍālēśvara, arirāyaravibhāḍa,bhāshaikku-tappuvarāyaragaṇḍa, mūvarāyara-ganḍa, ganḍara-ganḍa, ...ḍai-pratāpan, kaṭhāri-śāḷuvan,* he who took the countries that came in his sight and having once taken them never relinquished them afterwards, he who himself riding on a single horse took a herd of horses (from his enemies), he who bought credit to the two families (those of his father and mother), he who took all the countries, the king of kings who levied tribute on Īḻam (Ceylon), *rājamārttāṇḍan, rājakaṇṭhiravan,* the lord of kings, *kōṭṭattu-ma(va)nniyar ganḍan* (the dread to the enemies, *vanniyar,* in the *kōṭṭam*) a sun to the *Śori-manniyar,* a god of death to the *geḍi-manniyar, Tuṅgābhirāman, Durga-rēvantan,* a dread to those who . . . . on the sight of the army, an incarnation of the wielder of the five arrows (Kāma, the Hindu god of love), a disputer of disputants, *Tarkavinōdan*, a dread to those that come to collect (tribute ?), *Chaṇḍa-prachaṇḍan*, *Tuṅgābhirāman* (this and the next *biruda* are unnecessarily repeated here), *Durgarē-vantan*, the lord of the east, the south, the west and the north seas, Aśvapati, Gajapati and who was pleased to witness the dog-hunt,—when this king was ruling the kingdom of the world, in the year 1613 of the Śālivāhana Śaka era, on the 15th day of the month Tai of the year Dundubhi, we, the members of the *araiya* community who reside in the southern part of the village of Anbil which is situated in the Panṟiśūḻnāḍu, a sub-division of the Rājēndraśōḻavaḷanāḍu which is itself a division of the Rājarājanāḍu and hold service-tenure lands (in it) and who are the servants of Śrīmad-Vijayaraghunātharāya Toṇḍaimān, son of Śrīmat-Tirumalaiyappa Toṇḍaimān—all of us have given our consent to the conduct of the undermentioned charity and have given this copper-plate deed to Vēṅkaṭakṛishṇayyan, the son of Pavani Vēnkaṭayyan residing in the *uḻkaḍaippavani* in Kāñchipura.

(A levy has been fixed) at the rate of a *kuṟuṇi* of paddy per head per mensem on all those

No. VIII.

AN INSCRIPTION OF THE REIGN OF VIJAYARAṄGA-CHOKKANĀTHA NĀYANAYYAVĀRU : ŚAKA SAMVAT 1630.

THE subjoined inscription is also engraved on two sides of a single plate. This plate has got a projection on the top of semi-circular shape ; on the front side of this bit are engraved the sun and the moon, on the left and right respectively ; on the left a Liṅga is placed under a tree and worshipped by an elephant and a spider ; and on the right the figure of a standing Dēvī. Below the roots of the tree is a devotee seated cross legged and with hands folded across the chest in the *añjali* pose and below the Liṅga is a square divided into nine equal portions. There is absolutely no doubt in this case that the Liṅga represents the god Jambunātha and the goddess Akhilāṇḍēśvarī of the temple at Jambukēśvaram. The tree under which the Liṅga is represented is the Jambu tree peculiar to the temple of Jambukēśvaram (the *sthalavṛiksha*). The legend of this shrine is that an elephant and a spider worshipped daily the god Śiva at this place very devoutly and after its death the spider was reborn as the great Chōḷa king of the earlier times, Kō-ch-Cheṅgaṇṇāṇ. The devotee represents Jambu-muni from whose head, the sthala-purāṇa states, the Jambu tree sprang up and the nine squares perhaps stand for the tank Jambu-tīrtha in the temple. On the top of the first side of the plate and immediately below the figures described above, are engraved the words *Śrī Chandramauḷīśvarasvāmi.* The record belongs to the reign of the Nāyaka, king of Madhura, Vijaya-raṅga-Chokkanātha and is written in the Telugu characters and language. As is the characteristic feature with the inscriptions of this king's reign, the reduplication of consonants unnecessarily is met with in this one also; *e.g.*, in *manddu* in *ll.* 6, 7, 8 and 15; in *uṇḍḍagānu* in *l.* 9; in *koṇḍḍāṇ* in *l.* 15; in *vuṇḍḍeṭaṇdduna* in *l.* 17; in *naḍi-piñchcha* and *ājñāpiñchchi* in *l.* 18; in *maṅgalamllo* in *l.* 22; in *puramllo* and *jembbukēśvaram* in *l.* 28; in *śuṅkka* in. *l.* 32; in *vrāyiñchchi* in *l.* 33; and in *anubhaviñchchu* in *l.* 34. The inscription is dated the Śaka year 1630 corresponding to the cyclic year Vikṛiti.

In this year on Monday, the first *tithi* of the bright half of the month Kārttika, in the Rōhini

Nakshatra, the king Vijayaraṅga-Chokkanātha made a grant of lands situated in a number of places, at the instance of the then *svāmi* of the Śāradā Maṭha, for the maintenance of the feeding of Brāhmaṇas in the *maṭha* situated in the Poṇvāśikoṇḍāṇ street in Gajāraṇyakshētra. The following note has been kindly supplied to me by Mr. L.D. Swāmikkannu Pillai regarding the date:— " S. 1630. Vikṛiti, Kārttika Śukla 1, Induvāsara (Monday), Rōhini Nakshatra. Śukla, 1 *tithi* and Rōhiṇi Nakshatra cannot join together in Kārttika lunar month but may join in Jyēshṭha month. The date referred to was possibly Monday 10th May A.D. 1708 on which day Śukla 1 ended about sunrise—It was also a day of Rōhiṇi Nakshatra." The over-lord of the Madura Nāyaka mentioned in this document is said to be Vēṅkaṭadēva Mahārāya; he might perhaps be Raṅga *alias* Vēṅkaṭa given as the grandson of Vīra Vēṅkaṭa in the genealogical table appended to No. VI above. This Vēnkaṭadēva Mahārāya is said to have been reigning, seated on his jewelled throne in Ghanagiri, that is, Penugoṇḍa, his capital. Vijayaraṅga-Chokkanātha calls his own Government as the Dakshiṇasiṁhāsana and its rulers, the Dakshiṇa-siṁhāsanādhyakshas. The genealogy of the donor is given as follows:

Viśvanādha Nāyanivāru of the
Kāśyapa-gōtra, the
founder of the
dynasty.
|
Chokkanādha Nāyanivāru.
|
Raṅgakṛishṇa-Mudduvīrappa Nāyanivāru.
|
Vijayaraṅga-Chokkanādha Nāyanivāru.

The last king of the above table was also the last of the kings of the dynasty of the Madura Nāyakas. He was the grandson of the famous Maṅgammāḷ whose memory was fondly cherished by the people of the southern portion of the Madras Presidency and whose name and glory still lingers there. The earlier portion of this king's reign was under the efficient regency of his grand-mother Maṅgammāḷ, because his father died within seven years after his (father's) accession to the throne and Vijayaraṅga-Chokkanātha was a minor. When he himself died his queen Mīnākshī succeeded him; it was in this reign that Trichinopoly, the more important seat of the Government of the Madura Nāyakas, fell into the hands of the Nabobs of the Carnatic, by the machinations of their General Chanda Sahib.

The name of the *svāmi* of the Kāmākōṭi-Pīṭha at the time of this grant is not given; he is referred to only as Lōkaguru Śrīmad Śaṅkarāchārya-svāmulavāru. The plots of lands granted for the *annadāna kaṭṭaḷa* were situated in the following places:—in Mahēndramaṅgalam in the Toṭṭiyam-sīmā; in Kṛishṇāpuram; in Kārakkāḍu; in Koṇḍayampēṭṭai; in Maṅgamāmbāpuram in the Tiruchchendorai-sīmā; in Ariyūr in the Tinnam-sīmā and in Ariyamaṅgalam in the Kōnāḍu-sīmā. The document also records that certain dishes for *naivēdya* were to be prepared and offered daily to the god of the Jambukēśvaram temple; they are, cooked rice prepared from four *paḍis* of rice; *dōśē*, *atirasa*, *sugiyan* and *dipamchamaru* (oil for lamps); for this purpose the tolls collected on the two banks of the river (or the rivers Kāvērī and Koḷḷiḍam) were also assigned. The usual verses imploring the maintenance of the charity by the members of one's own race or those of other kings and the imprecatory verses are seen at the end, as also the signature of the king in big bold Telugu letters written by the king's own hand, as the document asserts.

The places mentioned in this inscription are: Gajāraṇyakshētram; Ponvāśikoṇḍān street in it; Toṭṭiyamsīmē and Mahēndramaṅgalam in it; Gōpālasvāmi's garden; Kṛishṇāpuram; Kārakkāḍu

Koṇḍayampēṭṭai, Tiruchchendoraisīmē and Maṅgammāpuram in it; Tinnamsīmē and Ariyalūr in it and Ariyamaṅgalam in the Kōnāḍusīmē. Of these, Gajāraṇyakshētram is another name for Jambukēśvaram or Tiruvaṇaikkāval. Which of the present streets of this town was known as the Ponvāśikoṇḍān street cannot be ascertained. The name Ponvaśikoṇḍān has reference to the history of the Śaiva Saint, Tirujñānasambandha ; when he and his elder contemporary Appar were obliged to stay away for a long time at Tiruvīḻimiḻalai on account of a severe famine that was then raging, the god of the temple of that place (Śiva) was pleased to grant to each of these devotees a gold piece a day for the maintenance of themselves and their dependents. The boy saint was fully conscious of his greatness, whereas the elderly saint never recognised any greatness in himself. So, the god, for the purpose of teaching better behaviour to the younger saint, was giving him a slightly debased coin, while he was systematically given a sound one to the elder. On account of the debasement in the coin, a small discount was always deducted by grocers when the money of Tirujñānasambandha was offered to them. On imploring the god to treat him equally with Apparsvāmigaḷ he obtained thenceforth sound coins. Toṭṭiyam-sīmē takes its name from the village

Toṭṭiyam in the Muśiri Tālūkā. This place has a large population of Telugu speaking Śūdras who are reputed to be masters of black-magic and are held in dread by the other people of the surrounding country. Mahēndramaṅgalam is on the bank of the river Kavērī opposite to Lālāppēṭṭai, a station on the Erode-Trichinopoly branch of the South Indian Railway and near the village of Śrīnivāsanallūr; the *maṭha* has still landed property here. There is a small stone shrine at Sannyāśi-maḍam, a hamlet of Mahēndramaṅgalam belonging to the Kumbhakōṇam maṭha, dedicated to Vēṇugōpālasvāmin. On the doorway of the shrine is carved a figure of an *advaiti sannyāsin* with his *daṇḍa* and *ghaṭa*. This temple and the adjoining lands are still in the possession of the Śaṅkarāchārya maṭha of Kumbhakōṇam. This shrine may be identified with the Gōpālasvāmin temple mentioned in the document. Kṛishṇāpuram is a village about half a mile to the east of Sannyaśi-māḍam. Kāraikkāḍu is some five miles west of Mahēndramaṅgalam in the Muśiri Tālūkā. Koṇḍayampēṭṭai is a suburb of Jambukēśvaram and Tiruchchendurai is a village situated 6 miles higher up Trichinopoly on the south bank of the Kavērī and has in it an ancient Śiva temple. It is not possible to identify Maṅgammāpuram. Tinnam-sīmē receives its name from the village of Tinniyam in the Trichinopoly Tālūkā and Ariyalūr is a town in the Uḍaiyārpāḷayam Tālūkā. The present Pudukkōṭṭai State and its surrounding country were known in ancient times as Kōnāḍu and Ariyamaṅgalam is a village very near Trichinopoly.

TEXT. [1]

FIRST SIDE.

१. श्रीचंद्रमौळीश्वरस्वामि [॥*]
२. श्रीमत्परमहंसपरिव्राजकाचार्यवर्य[2] श्रीकांचीपुर-
३. स्तित श्रीमच्छंकरभगवत्पादाचारय् स्वामुलवारिकि [॥]
४. [3]स्वास्ति श्रीविजयाभ्युदय शालिवाहन शकाब्दमुलु
५. १६३० अगुनेटि विक्रुतिनाम संवत्सरं कात्तिक शुध[4] १५ यिं-
६. द्दु[5]वासरं रोहिणिनक्षत्रं ई कूडिन शुभादिनमं-
७. द्दु[5][॥*] श्रीमद्राजाधिराज परमेश्वर वीरप्रताप श्रीवेंकट-
८. देवमहारायलय्यवारु घनगिरिनगरमंद्दु[5] रत्नसिं-
९. हासनासनुलै पृथ्विसांम्राज्यं शेयुचुनुंड्ड[6]गानु

---

1. From the inked impressions.
2. वर्य is engraved above the line.
3. There is some space left between lines 3 & 4.
4. Read कार्तिकशुद्ध०:
5. Read इन्दु: wherever द is doubled read it simply as द (with its secondary forms).
6. Read ०नुण्ड०: wherever ड is doubled, read it simply as ड.

cription of Vijayaraṅga Chokkanātha Nāyanayyavāru, Śaka Samvat, 1630, No. VIII.

Ia

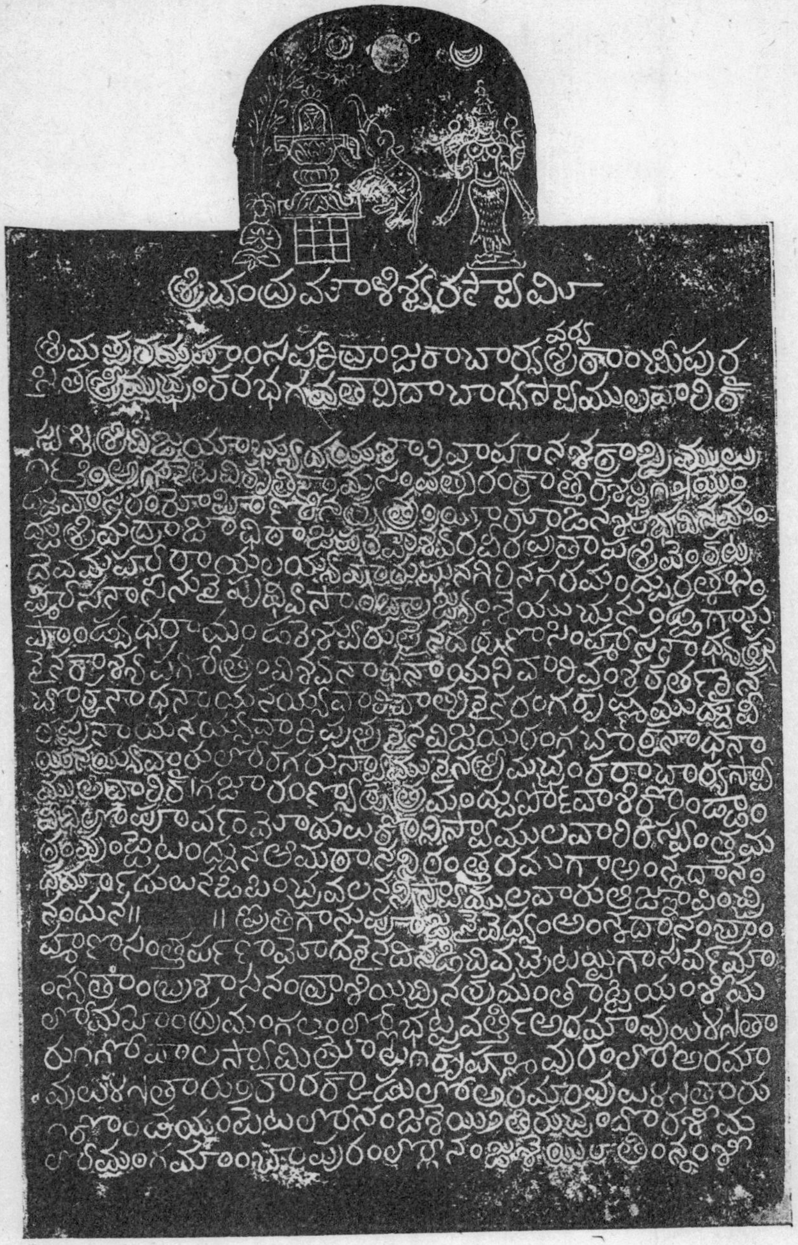

SCALE O. 7.

T. A. GOPINATHA RAO.

Half-Tone by Photo-Engraving Co., Madras.

१०. पांड्यधरामंडलेश्वरु[लै]न दक्षिणसिंह्मा[8]सनाध्यक्षु-

११. लैन काश्यपगोत्रं विश्वनाध[9]नायनिवारि वंशकर्तलैन

१२. चोक्कनाध[9]नायनय्यवारि पौतृलैन[10] रंगकृष्णमुद्दुवी-

१३. रप्पनायनय्यवारि पुतृलैन[10] विजयरंगचोक्कनाधना[9]-

१४. यनय्यवारु लोकगुरुस्वामुलैन श्रीमच्छंकराचार्‌यस्वा-

१५. मुलवारिकि । गजारण्यक्षेत्रमंदु[5] पोनूवाशिकोंड्डां[6]

१६. वीधिलो पूर्व मोदुल्लुकोनि स्वामुलवारिकि स्वंत्त[7]म-

१७. ठवुंड्डे[6]टंदुन[5] आ मठाान निरंत्त[7]रमुगा अंन्नदानं[11]

१८. धर्मादुलु नडिपिंच्च[12]वलननि स्वामुलवारु आज्ञापिंचि[12]-

१९. नंदुन ॥ ॥ प्रीतिगानु पूजनैवेद्यं अंन्नदानं[11]ब्रां-

२०. ह्मण[13]संत्त[7]र्पणमोदलैनदि नडिचिवच्चेटट्टुगा सर्वमां-

२१. न्यतांब्रशासनं[14] व्राशि यिच्चिन क्रमं [॥*] तोट्टियं शीम-

२२. लो महेंन्द्रमंगलंल्लो[15] भट्टवर्त्ति[16]अरमावु ६४१ [17] ता

२३. रु १ [।*] गोपालस्वामि तोट १ [।*] कृष्णापुरंलो अरमा-

२४. वु ६४१ [17]तारु २[।*] कारक्काडुलो अरमावु ६४१ [17] तारु

---

7. Read स्वन्त: wherever त is doubled, read it simply as त.

8. Read सिंहासना०.

9. Read ०नाथ.

10. Read पौत्रुलैन and पुत्रुलैन

11. Read अन्नदानं

12. Read आज्ञापिंचि: read the doubled च simply as च

13. Read ब्राह्मण०

14. Read ताम्र०.

15. Read ०मंगलंलो read the doubled ल simply as ल.

16. Read भट्टवृत्ति

17. A numerical symbol is used here, which is not reproduced in the transcript.

२५. १ [।*] कोंडयं पेटलो नंज शेयि २ [।*] तिरुचंदोरशीम-

२६. लो मंगमांबापुरंह्लो[15]नंज शेयि ८ [।*] तिंन्नंशी[18]-

SECOND SIDE.

२७. मलो अरियूरुलो नंज शेयि १६ [।*] दक्षिणं कोना-

२८. डुशीमलो अरियमंगलंह्लो[15]नंज शेयि ६ [॥*] जेंब्बुकेश्व[19]-

२९. रंगुडलो[20]नित्य कट्टड[21]दिनं[22] १ कि बिय्यं पडि ४ अंन्नं[11] तळिगल्लु

३०. २[।*] दोशलु २ [।*] अतिरसाल्लु २ [।*]सुगिय १ [।*] दीपं चमरु प[डि ?] ९ [17][॥*] वुभ-

३१. य तीरंलोनु शेयि १ कि तूमुदुवडुवंत्तुनानुंन्नु[23]

३२. सुंकान नित्य कट्टडगग[21] १ [॥*] यी प्रकारं नडिचि- वच्चेटगा

३३. दिट्टंचेशि व्रायिंचि[12]नामुगनक तामुंन्नु[24]पठपरं[25]-

३४. प्परलगा अनुभविंन्चु[12]कोनि आचें[26]द्रार्क स्थायिगा धर्म-

३५. परिपालनं चेसुकोमुचु आशीर्वादं शायगलदि ॥ दान-

३६. पालनयोर्मध्ये दानाच्छ्रे[27]योनुपालनं । दानात्स्व-

---

18. Read तिन्नियं

19. Read जम्बुकेश्वरं

20. Read गुडिलो

21. कट्टड is a corruption of the Tamil word kattalai.

22. The word दिनं is written in the original as द्रिं.

23. Read ०वंतुनानुन्नु

24. Read तामुन्नु

25. Read पट्टपरंपर

26. Read आचन्द्रार्क

27. Read दानाचाच्छ्रे०.

cription of Vijayaraṅga Chokkanātha Nāyanayyavāru, Śaka Samvat 1630, No. VIII.

Ib

SCALE O. 7.

T. A. GOPINATHA RAO. Half-Tone by Photo-Engraving Co., Madras.

३७. र्गमवाप्नोति पालनादच्चुतं[28]पदं ॥ स्वदत्ताद्विगुणं

३८. पुंण्यं परदत्तानुपालनं । परदत्तापहारेण स्वद-

३९. त्तं निष्पलं[29]भवेत् ॥ स्वदत्तां परदत्तां वा यो हरे-

४०. त वसुंद्धरा[30] षर्ष्टिवर्षसहस्राणि[31] विष्टायां जाय-

४१. ते क्रिमिः ॥ मद्वंशजाः परमहिपतिवंशजा वा ये

४२. भूमिपा(:)स्सततमुज्वलधर्मचित्ताः । मद्धर्ममेव

४३. परिपालनमाचरंत्ति[7] तत्पादुकाद्वयमहं शिर-

४४. सा वहामि ॥

४५. विजयरंगच्चोक्कना-

४६. धनायनय्य व्राळ्ळु [॥*]

ABSTRACT OF CONTENTS.

Line 1. (Invocation to the god). Śrīchandramauḷēśvarasvāmi (the aspect of Śiva worshipped in the Śaṅkārachārya maṭha of both Kumbhakōṇam and Śriṅgēri and all other Śaṅkarāchārya maṭhas).

Ll. 2-3. To Śaṅkarabhagavatpādāchāryasvāmin, who is a *paramahaṁsa*, the highest among the *parivrājaka-āchāryas* and who resides at Kañchipura :

---

28. Read ०दच्युतं.

29. Read निष्फलं.

30. Read वसुन्धराम्.

31. Read षष्टिं and विष्ठायां.

Ll. 4-6. Be it well! In the victorious era of Śālivāhana, the year 1630 being current, on the Monday which corresponded with the 15th *tithi* of the bright fortnight of the month Kārttika, and nakshatra Rōhiṇī, in the year Vikriti :

Ll. 6-9. On this auspicious day, while Veṅkaṭadēvamahārāya who bore the imperial titles *rājādhirāja*, *paramēśvara* and *vīra-pratāpa*, being seated upon the jewelled throne at Ghanagiri (Penukoṇḍa), was ruling the kingdom of the world.

Ll. 10-15. Vijaya-Raṅga-Chokkanātha-Nāyanayyavāru, the son of Raṅga-Kṛishṇa-Mudduvīrappa-Nāyanayyavāru and the grandson of Chokkanātha-Nāyanayyavāru who was the perpetuator of the race of Viśvanātha-Nāyanivaru, who belonged to the Kaśyapa gōtra and who was the Lord of the Pāṇḍyamaṇḍala and the rightful occupant of the southern *simhāsana* (the southern kingdom, that is, the Madura Nāyakdom), gave to Śaṅkarāchāryasvāmi, who is the preceptor of the world (*lōkaguru*) the following:

Ll. 15-19. The *svāmin* having his own *maṭha*, from olden times, situated in the Ponvāśikoṇḍān street in the Gājaraṇyakshētra (Jambukēśvara, Tiruvānaikkā near Srīraṅgam) commanded (us) that in that *maṭha* charities such as feeding (*annādana*) etc., should be conducted perpetually.

Ll. 19-21.—(Thereon the following order was issued on a copper-plate embodying the freehold lands granted for the conduct of the *pūjā*, *naivēdya* (food offering), feeding to the satisfaction of brāhmaṇas, &c.

Ll. 21-28.—4½ half *mās* with one *tāru* of land belonging to the *bhaṭṭavṛitti* (land) in (the village of) Mahēndramaṅgalam situated in the Toṭṭiyam-sīmē; the garden of Gōpālasvāmin 1; 4½ half *mās* with two *tārus* of land in Kṛishṇāpuram; 4½ half *mās* with one *tāru* in Kārakkāḍu; 2 *śeys* of wet land in Koṇḍayampēṭṭai; 8 *śeys* of wet land in (the village of) Maṅgamāmbāpuram situated in the Tiruchchendorai-sīmē; 16 *śeys* of wet land in Ariyūr situated in the Tinniyam-sīmē; and 6 *śeys* of wet land in the village of Ariyamaṅgalam situated in the Kōnāḍu-sīmē in the south.

Ll. 28-32.—For the daily offerings consisting of 4 paḍis (measures of uncooked rice) 2 *taḻigais* of cooked rice, 2 *dōśais*, 2 *atirasams*, 1 *sigiyan*, and ¾ padi of oil (for lamp), to be offered to the god in the temple of Jambukēśvaram, the following were given, namely, *śēys* (of land) on either bank (of the river Kāveri), as also the tolls (here, a portion of the passage is somewhat obscure).

Ll. 32.—We have made these arrangements, in accordance with which the deed was also written, so that (the charity) might be conducted in this (aforesaid) manner; you and your line of disciples shall also enjoy (the lands), shall conduct the charities as long as the sun and the moon subsist and grant us your blessings.

(Then follow the four common verses conveying the virtues of the protection of charities and imploring the subsequent generation of kings to protect this charity).

No. IX.

A FIRMĀN BY THE EMPEROR OF DELHI (?).

HIJIRA 1088.

THE inscription edited below is a *firmān* issued in favour of His Holiness, the Svāmi Paramahaṁsa Parivrājakāchārya of the Śāradā maṭha in the sacred place of Kāñchi, otherwise known as the Satyavratakshētra, embodying in it an annual *inām* of 115 *varāhas*, meant for the purposes of worship and daily offerings to the god Chandramauḷīśvara and for the feeding of Brāhmaṇas. The grantor of the *inām* is described as 'an Emperor who is obeyed by all the world, who is a Sultan upon whom all the mahārājas depend and who is the representative of god on earth.'

The inscription is written in the Telugu alphabet; the first part of the record which is engraved on the first side of the first plate is in the Saṅskṛit language; the second part beginning from *l.* 13 up to *l.* 27 is in the Persian language; the third part, from *ll.* 27 to 39 which embodies the *praśasti* of the *svāmis* of the Śāradā-maṭha, is once again in Saṅskṛit; then, the fourth part, from *ll.* 40 to 47 is in the Telugu language; the last and the fifth part is again in Persian. The inscription is dated the 1st of the month Shauval of the year 1088 of the Hijira Era, which is equivalent to 1710 A.D. In A.D. 1707, the great Moghul Emperor Aurangazib died and was succeeded by Bahadur Shah, but the latter died in an attempt to put down the Sikhs at Lahore in 1712. The date of our firmān falls within the reign of this Emperor, who is said to have been a wise and valiant prince, and as such might very likely have made the grant of the *inām* to the *svāmi* of the Śāradā-maṭha of Kāñchi. But the document is silent about the actual name of the Emperor who ordered the *inām* to be given to the *maṭha* and therefore we may believe that it was perhaps issued by Bahadur Shah. The order is addressed to the village officers, villagers and the tax-gatherers in Changalpaṭṭu division; the person who made a representation to the imperial Court for the granting of this *inam* was Liṅgōji Sangarsu, the Tarafdār (collector of revenue) of the district of Mēlpāka belonging to the Changalpaṭṭu jurisdiction; at the

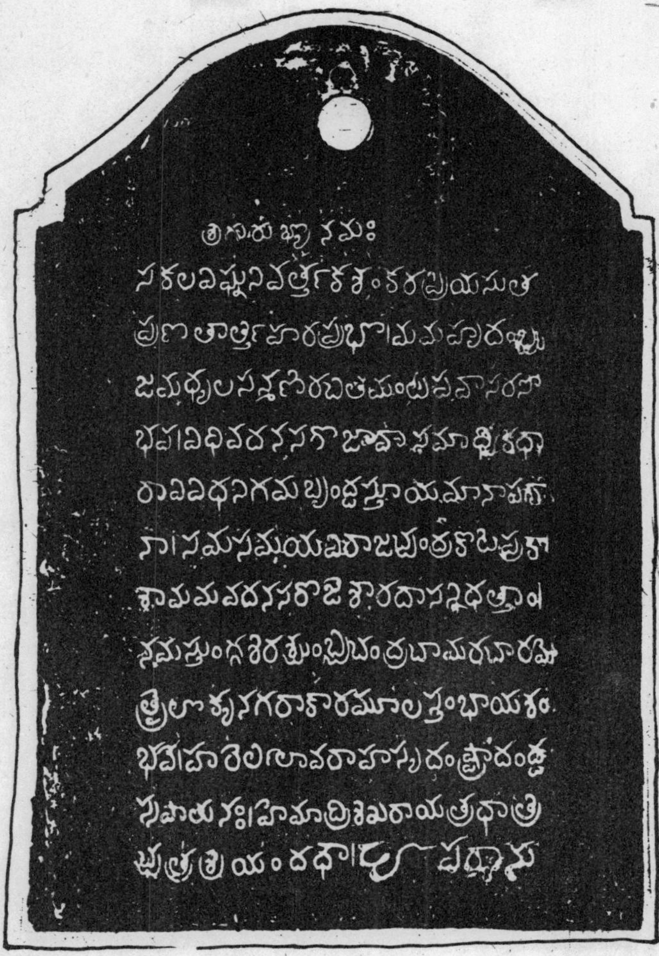

శ్రీ గురుభ్యో నమః
సకలవిఘ్ననివర్త్తక శంకరప్రియసుత
ప్రణతార్త్తిహరప్రభో। మమహృదబ్జ
జమధ్యలసన్మణిరచితమంటపవాసరసో
భవ। విధివదనసరోజావాసమాధ్వీకధా
రావివిధనిగమబృందస్తూయమానాపఘ్న
నా। సమస్తసమయవిరాజచ్చంద్రకోటిప్రకా
శామమవదనసరోజె శారదాసన్నిధత్తాం॥
నమస్తుంగశిరశ్చుంబిచంద్రచామరచారవే
త్రైలోక్యనగరారంభమూలస్తంభాయశం
భవే॥ హరేర్లీలావరాహస్య దంష్ట్రాదండ
స్సపాతునః॥ హేమాద్రికలశాయత్రధాత్రి
ఛత్రశ్రియందధౌ। [illegible] పర్థాను

end of the record is the signature of Tamada Bhānuji, the District Revenue Accountant.

The village Mēlpākkam mentioned in the inscription is situated in the Madhurāntakam Talūka of the Chingleput District.

I am indebted to Prof. K. Amṛita Rao, M. A., the polyglot scholar and eminent philologist, for the translation of and notes on this copper-plate grant, and I take this opportunity to offer him my grateful thanks for the trouble he has taken on my account.

TEXT [1].

FIRST PLATE, SECOND SIDE.

श्रीगुरुभ्यो नमः

१. सकलविघ्ननिवर्त्तक[3] शंकरप्रियसुत
२. प्रणतार्त्तिहर[4]प्रभो । मम हृदंब्बु[5]-
३. जमध्यलसन्मणिरचितमंटप[6]वासरसो
४. भव । विधवदनसरोजावासमाध्विकधा[7]-
५. राविविधानिगम[8]बृंदस्तूयमानापदा-
६. ना । समसमयविराजच्चंद्रकोटिप्रका-
७. शा मम वदनसरोजे शारदा सन्निधत्तां ।[2]

---

1. From the original and the impressions.
2. These two *ślōkas* occur in a work called the *Śivāshṭapadī* of one Chandraśēkharēndra Sarasvati, one of the pontiffs of the Kāmakōṭi *pīṭha*.
3. For निवर्त्तक Read निवर्तक
4. „ प्रणतार्त्ति „ प्रणतार्ति
5. „ हृदंब्बु „ हृदंबु
6. „ मंटप „ मंडप
7. „ ॰माध्विक „ माध्वीकं
8. „ बृंद „ बृन्द

८. नमस्तुंग्गशिर(।)श्चुंब्वि[9]चंद्रचामरचारवे ।
९. त्रैलोक्यनगराकारमूलस्तंभाय शं-
१०. भवे । हरेर्लीलावराहस्य दंष्ट्रादंड्ड-[10]
११. स्स पातु नः । हेमाद्रिशिखरा यत्र धात्रि*

SECOND PLATE, FIRST SIDE.

१२. च्छत्रश्रियं दधौ । पर्मांनु
१३. परानुजहामता[11]आफ्तबे यिर्तिफा
१४. वाजिबुल यित्तिबा अजदिवानु ह्र-
१५. मायुनु[12]खेलाफतमशहूनुमै
१६. मनत[13]मकरूनु चिना शरप्स

---

9. „ ०श्चुंब्वि „ श्चुंबि
10. „ दंड्ड „ दंड
* „ धात्रि „ धात्री
11. पर्मांनु परानु जहामता should be farmān-farmāi jahān-mutā, *i.e.*, an issuer of orders (monarch, emperor, who is obeyed by the whole world).
पर्मांनु परानु....यिनिवा refers to the Emperor.
अज दिवानु....from the office of such an Emperor.
आफ्तबे, of the sun.
यिर्तिफा, at the zenith.
वाजिबुल यित्तिबा, who deserves to be obeyed.
12. दिवानु हुमायुनु should be written dīwāni humāyūm: The august or imperial Court. खेलाफत, Caliphate, imperial dignity, monarchy. मशहूनु, filled, charged with.
13. मैमनत मकरूनु, august, *e.g.*, nama'i humāyūm maimanat maqrūn means an august, imperial, royal letter. चिना, thus. शरप्स सुदूरु promulgated, issued with dignity. स is unnecessary in शरप्सः, we should have शरफ.

A Firman of the Emperor of Delhi (?), No. IX.

IIa.

SCALE O. 6.

. A. GOPINATHA RAO.

Half-Tone by Photo-Engraving Co., Madras.

१७. सुदूरू व यिजज्जुहुरु याप्त[14]

१८. के । कारुकु नानि[15]व मादलारि

१९. यानि व नाट्टुवारानि[16]व कापलि

२०. कारानि व मोकधमानि[17]वरया

२१. नि व कुलकरिणियानि ह(।)ल्लुप

२२. यिस्तक चाल्लु[18]वल्लं मागाण अ

२३. मालिमा[19] चंग्गालिपट्टु बिदा

२४. नंदके[20] । म[21] ।। मेलु पाक अमा

---

14. यिजज्जुहुरुयाप्त (प्त) = same as शरप्स सुदूरु.

15. कारुकुनानि, clerks. मादलारियानि, *modalalu*, a chief or headman, mudalāli, a president, a proprietor. Mudali, a title of agricultural and some other respectable class. I think मादलारियानि may be taken as respectable people of the village.

16. नाट्टुवारानि, villagers, कापलिकारानि, agriculturists.

17. मोकधमानि, Mokaddam, the head of a village or caste. रयानि, farmers, कुलकर्णियानि, village accountants.

18. हल्लुप यिस्तक चाल्लु should be हाल्व यिस्तबाल्, *i.e.*, present and future. वल्लं, I think should be पल्ल. *Māgāṇi*, a division of a revenue district usually consisting of 6 or 7 villages; the subdivision of a tahsildari. It also means wet cultivation. This meaning suits the context on account of पल्ल.

19. अमालिमा, artificers, artisans, workmen, agents; *tax-gatherers*: governors, rulers, notably *tax-gatherers* suits the context.

20. बिदानंदके, let them know that.

21. म is redundant.

२५. लि माघाण मज्कूरु रु[22] अर्जु

२६. दास्तु[23]लिंग्गो जि संग्गर्सु तर

SECOND PLATE, SECOND SIDE.

२७. पुदारुहे[24] नूटपधेनु

२८. वरहाल्कु [||*] स्वस्तिाश्रि[25]मदखिल भूमं-

२९. डलालंक्कार[26]त्रयस्त्रिंशत्कोटि-

३०. देवतासेवित श्रि[25] कामाक्षिदेवि सना-

३१. ध[27]श्रि[25]मदेकांम्रनाध[28]साक्षात्कार प-

३२. रमाधिष्टान कृतदि चतुर्युग-

३३. सकल धांर्मिक[29]राजपरिपालि-

३४. त सकल वेदशास्त्र मूल भूत-

३५. सत्यव्रतनामांक्किकत[30]कांञ्चि[31]दि-

३६. व्यक्षेत्रे शारदामठसंस्तित्त[32]श्रि-[25]

---

22. मज्कूरु रु: रु. is redundant.

23. अर्जुदास्तु, petition, representation.

24. तरपुदारुहे, *Tarafdar*, is an officer of Government in charge of a *Taraf*, (firkah, division of a taluq), collecting the revenue and exercising chief revenue and police authority in his district. It also means—The holder of a taraf-portion of village lands.

25. For श्रि Read श्री, also in lines 30, 31, 36, 38, 39.

26. For भूमंड्डलालंकार Read भूमंडलालंकार

27. For सनाध Read सनाथ

28. ,, एकांम्रनाध ,, एकाम्रनाथ

29. ,, धांर्मिक ,, धार्मिक

30. ,, नामांक्कित ,, नामांकित

31. ,, कांञ्चि ,, कांची

32. ,, संस्तित्त ,, संस्थित

A Firman of the Emperor of Delhi (?), No. IX.

SCALE O. 6.

A. GOPINATHA RAO. Half-Tone by Photo-Engraving Co., Madras.

३७. मत्परमहंसप्ररिव्राजका-
३८. चार्यश्रि[35]शंक्कराचार्यमाजि-[33]
३९. त श्रि [25]चंद्र मवुळिश्वर स्वामिकि

THIRD PLATE, FIRST SIDE.

४०. दिपाराधन नित्य नैवेद्य ब्रांह्म[34]-
४१. ण समाराधन मोदलैन सकल वि-
४२. ध पूजार्ध[35]गानु । यिनामु कट्टड
४३. चेशिनारं अदिगनक निराछेदन-
४४. गा साल्लु बस्साल्लु स्वामिकि यि-
४५. नां नडि पिं स्तू वच्चेदि ता
४६. लिकु ब्राशी पुच्चुकोनि अस्लि[36] पर
४७. मानु तिर्गा यिच्चेदि च मा १
४८. हे सव्वाल्लु स
४९. न १०८८-४
५०. पर्वा
५१. न्गिमो कर्र बुल
५२. हजरतुल खाका
५३. नि[36]मोत मिनु डाल तु

33. For शंक्करा Read शंकरा
माजित ,, पूजित

34. ,, ब्रांह्म० ,, ब्राह्म०

35. ,, पूजार्ध ,, पूजार्थे

36. अस्लि—original.

I cannot understand the symbol after 1088; 1st of Shauwal 1088 Higira.

Shauwal, the tenth Muhammadan month, beginning with the Bairam feast or break of the fast of Ramazan.

36. परवान्गि = permission.

मोकरिबुल् हजरतुल खाकानि

मोकरिबुल् near, of one who is near (minister).

५४. ल सुलुतानि मज्मु अ
५५. अतुवाके[37]हवाखो हे मह(ा)
५६. रजह(ा) न वाके जिल्लु यिल्लु[38] यिला
५७. त्ता मादा भानु जि मज्मु अ
५८. दारु[39]शाहो

हजरतुल of the presence.
खाकानि of the King-Emperor.
permission from near the presence or of the minister, *i. e.*, King's order issued from the imperial Court. मोतामिजुद्दाल्तु should b eमोतामिजुद्दवल्तु protector of the Kingdom.

37. मज्मुअतुवाके *Majma*, a place of assembly, a concourse, crowd, meeting.
tawaqqu hope, desire; reliance, expectation.
tauq (v.n.) a necklace, chain, collar, a ring, a circle round anything. We may therefore take it in three ways the Emperor, at whose court the whole circle (*i. e.*, all) the (tributary) Mahārājas meet, *or* the Emperor, in whom the hopes of all the Mahārājas are centred, or on whom all the Mahārājas place their reliances, *i.e.*, depend.

38. जिल्लु यिल्लु यिला zillu'l-lah, the shadow or representative of God (a royal title or epithet).

39. *Majmua-dār.* In Tamil countries, a district revenue accountant. Generally, he is a native revenue-accountant, who keeps the account of the Jama or Government collections under the native governments. In Hindustan he was the revenue-accountant of a District, subordinate to the Amil or manager and removable at pleasure. In Mahratha finance the Majumdar was a kind of Auditor whose function it was to *inscribe all writs and deeds* and to write on all accounts of receipts and disbursements after examination. *In Gujerat*, keepers of revenue records.
Mujumoodār. The Head-Accountant of a Taluq Cutcherry.

A Firman of the Emperor of Delhi (?), No. IX.

IIIa

SCALE O. 6.

A FIRMĀN BY THE EMPEROR OF DELHI.

TRANSLATION.*

Salutation to the preceptors!

"Oh Lord, who is the beloved son of Śaṅkara, the remover of all obstacles (difficulties) and the dispeller of the sorrows of those who bow down to thee; take a delight in residing (be pleased to reside) in the *maṇḍapa* (temple) made of brilliant gems in the middle of my lotus-like heart. May Śāradā reside in my lotus-like mouth, Śāradā, who is, as it were, the stream of honey flowing from the lotus-like face of Brahmā, Śāradā, whose actions (glorious utterances) are praised by the several Vēdas and whose lustre equals that of crores of moons shining simultaneously. Reverence to Śambhu, who is rendered beautiful by a chowri, which is the moon that lightly rests upon his lofty head, and who is the pillar of foundation for building 'the city of the three worlds'. Let the tusk of the boar of amusement of Hari protect us, on account of which tusk, the earth looked like a beautiful umbrella on the top of Mount Sumēru.

Firmān issued (with honour and dignity) under the authority of the august and imperial government of an Emperor, who is obeyed by all the

* By Prof. K. Amrita Rao, M.A.

world, and who resembles the sun at his zenith and is worthy of being obeyed.

Let the clerks, landed proprietors, villagers, agriculturists, headmen of villages, farmers, village karṇams, the present and future tax-gatherers of wet lands of Chaṅgalpaṭṭu hereby know that on the representation (petition) of Liṅgōji Saṅgarsu, Taraf-dar (collector of revenue of the district) of Mēlpāka, belonging to the aforesaid jurisdiction, we have ordered an inam of 115 varāhas to be granted for purposes of worship (waving lights before the idol), daily offerings of cakes &c., and all other kinds of worship such as feeding of Brāhmaṇas, to god Chandramauḷīśvara, worshipped by his Holiness Svāmi Paramahaṁsa Prarivrājakāchārya of Śāradā *maṭha* in the sacred place of Kāñchi, otherwise called Satyavrata, the source of all Vēdas and Śāstras, patronised by all the beneficent kings of the four ages beginning with Kṛita-yuga, a sacred place, where Śri Ēkāmranātha, the consort of Śrī Kāmākshī, served by 33 crores of gods, who are the ornament of the earth, chose to reveal himself. The *inām* amount, therefore should be paid to the God, every year, without fail. A copy should be made and the original firmān should be returned : 1st of Shauval 1088.

Order issued from the court of the Emperor,

who is the protector of the Empire, a Sultān upon whom all the mahārājahs who are the well-wishers of the Empire depend, and who is the representative of God on earth. Tamada Bhanuji, District Revenue Accountant."

No. X.

AN INSCRIPTION OF ŚAKA SAMVAT 1608.

THE subjoined inscription is engraved on two sides of a single plate in an extremely slipshod manner and in a kind of Nāgari character which is quite modern and which is very peculiar for the shapes of the letters and it is full of mistakes. The first part of the inscription from *l*. 1 to *l*. 3 is in the Telugu language; then comes the Sanskṛit *praśasti* of the *Svāmis* of the Śāradā-maṭha of Kāñchi and cover *ll*. 3 to 15 and the rest of the document is in Telugu.

The inscription is dated Saturday, the 15th *tithi* of the bright half of the month Vaiśākha, in the year Prabhava which corresponded with the Śaka year 1608. On this day there occurred an eclipse of the moon; on this *puṇyakāla*, Mahadēvēndra Sarasvati, disciple of Chandraśēkhara Sarasvati of the Śāradā-maṭha of Kāñchi gave to a brāhmaṇa named Rāma Śāstri who belonged to the

Hoysaṇa Karṇāṭa sect (*i.e.*, the Karṇātakas of the Hoysaḷa country, one of the sub-division of the Karṇāṭakas) and of the Āśvalāyana sūtra and Kāmakāyana Viśvāmitra gōtra, land in the village of Mēlupākkam and some taxes, two *varāhas* per annum from the *maṭha*, and two house-sites. The village of Mēlupāka belonged to the Jāghīr-sīmē granted to the maṭha in the Chaṅgalpaṭṭu jurisdiction sometime before the date of our record by the brothers Akkanna and Mādanna of Gōlakoṇḍa. As regards the date, Mr. L. D. Swamikkannu Pillai writes as follows.—"Ś 1608, Prabhava, Viśākha, Śudi. 15, Saturday, lunar eclipse. Ś 1608 A.D. =1686-87; but Prabhava was A.D. 1687-88. The day intended was Saturday, 16th April, A.D. 1687. The *tithi* commenced at ·58 of the day and ended at ·55 of the following day. There was no lunar eclipse on the day in question." The brothers Akkanna and Mādanna mentioned in the inscription under notice were the ministers of the Kuṭb Shāhi Sultān, Abul Hāsan. They are also said to be the uncles of the devotee Rāmadāsa, who is believed by people to have held the Tahsildāri of Bhadrāchalam and who was put to torture for embezzlement of the public revenue, for the purpose of building a temple for the god Rāma and endowing it. Abul Hāsan, the last of the Sultāns of Gōlkonda, is said to have confided the conduct of the affairs of his Government to these brāhmaṇa ministers and was himself enjoying life. The following account of these two persons is taken from the Madras Epigraphist's Annual Report for 1915. "The Dutch journalist Havart supplies some information about Akkanna and Mādanna, the ministers of the Kuṭb Shāhi kings, Abdulla Kuṭb Shāh and Abul Hāsan. They were two brothers born of a very poor family who entered service as shroffs in A.D. 1666 on a pay of 10 *gilders* per mensem under Saiyyad Mustapha, a nobleman of Gōlkoṇḍa known to fame as Mir Zumla. Mādanna *alias* Sūryaprakāśa Rao is stated by the Dutch journalist to have been an intelligent man whereas his brother Akkanna was a man of cunning and roguery with very little of understanding. The brothers rose in rank by an apparent act of treachery which cost Mir Zumla his high office under the Nabobs of Gōlkoṇḍa. Mādanna became a very prominent figure in the administration of the kingdom so much so that the Sultān left everything to his care and was satisfied with receiving 75,000 dollars for his personal use. Mādanna was well versed in Persian, Hindustani and the Vernaculars of the country and lived in a kingly style. As the golden palanquin in which he went out, passed in

Havart on Akkanna and Madanna

the streets, people showed their respect by stopping on the way. He was very kind to the Dutch and the author of the journal, Havart, says that he had the honour of seeing Mādanna often.

"Having served under Abdulla Kuṭb Shāh (A.D. 1611-72) the two brothers seem to have maintained the same high position also under the reign of Abul Hāsan, the successor of Abdulla Kuṭb Shāh. But they were not to maintain this long. In A.D. 1685 the Mughal king, Aurangazeb marched with his army into Gōlkoṇḍa and plundered first the house of Mādanna. The people were in a state of panic and accused Mādanna of high treason. Under orders from the Sultān they murdered the two brothers who were once the bosom friends of the king, in a most ignominious way. Akkanna and Mādanna were dragged along the streets in the presence of the people (fig. d. on Plate II). The head of Mādanna was severed from the body and sent to Aurangazeb while that of Akkanna was trampled under the foot of an elephant. The death of the two brothers must have happened after the 29th of October 1685 when the Mughal army entered Gōlkoṇḍa and perhaps before the end of that month. The Sultān Abul Hāsan who thought that he would now be safe was himself deposed and confined in Daulatabad in 1687."

Sultan Abul-Hassan Kutb Shah,

Madanna Suryaprakasa Rau,

Four pictures are reproduced from Havart's Journal. Under each one of the pictures, Havart has affixed a short passage in the Dutch language giving an estimate of each of the personages depicted there. They run as follows:—

PLATE II.

Tweede deel, Fol. 219=Second Volume, p. 219.

Akkanna and Mādanna.

Sultaan Aboe-il-Hassan Kotbsiah Konig van Golkonda,=Sultan Abu-l-Hassan Kutbshah, King of Golkonda.

Nemo felix ntae obitum=No one is happy before his death.

Hy was een Koning in de naam, niot in der daad.

Quam tot die waardigheit van de alderlaagste staat.

En liet don andere, zig zelf, ent Ryk bestieren.

Een dom, onnozel Mensch, niet Vorstlyk in manieren.

Toen nu't qeluk met hem een tyd lang had gefopt (?)

Wierd hy don Eygen Schuld van Kroon En Throon geschopt.

Kroop in het zant, vrat stof, moest zich als
slaaf Vermindren.
Wee Zulken land alwaar de Koningen Zyn
Kind'ren.

TRANSLATION.

He was a king (only) in name, (and) not in deed (actually). He attained to that dignity from the very lowest position and allowed himself and his kingdom to be governed by others. He was a stupid and silly man, and not kingly in manners (never behaved like a king). When now fortune had fooled with him a long time, he was kicked from (deprived of) his crown and throne by his own fault. He crept in the sand, ate dust, and had to humiliate himself (behave) like a slave. Woe to that country where kings are (mere) children.

D. HAVART.

Tweede deel, Fol. 219=
Second Volume, p. 219.

Mādoena Sureparkaas Row Albestierder van het Golcondeze Ryk = Mādanna Suryaprakas Rao, All-Governor (Regent, Prime Minister, etc.,) of the Golcondian Empire.

Akkanna, The Commander-in-chief

The bodies of Akkanna and Madanna

Hier Zietmen Mādoena naar't leven afgetekend,
Die van den eersten tyd Zyns Ionkheyds afgerekend,
Tot aan Zyn dood toe was een speel-kind vant' geluk:
Hy is van niet tot zoo een hoogen trap verheven,
Dat zelf de Konink naar Zyn wenk heest moeten leven:
Hy heest Zyn Eygen Heer (O heylloos schellemsteek!)
Van ampt, en staat gezet, ja alles derven wagen,
Maar tragtende Zyn Vorst levren in de hand,
Des vyands, raakte hy, toen't uytquam aan een Kant,
Door sidemaktas swaard, teynd moet de last tog dragem.

(TRANSLATION).

Here we see Mādanna drawn to life, who was the play thing of fortune from the beginning of his youth until his death. He has risen from nothing to such a high level that even the king must obey him. He has removed his own master from office and state (O sacrilegious act of scoundrelism!)

Nay, he dared to do anything. But, while attempting to deliver his king into the hands of the enemy he was discovered and lost his life through Sidemakta's sword. In the end, after all the burden must be borne.

D. HAVART.

Tollantur in altum ut lapsu graviore ruant-Let them be borne on high that they may rush to their fall more heavily.

Tweede deel, Fol. 220-
Second Volume, p. 220.

Akkana Opper-boekhouder en Generalissimus von het Golcondaze Leger-.

Akkanna Upper-bookkeeper (senior Accountant) and Supreme General of the Golcondian Army.

Alter idem-the second, the same.

Hier Zietmen in het kleyn de schets van Akkana.

Een beest in menschen schyn : wiens loze boze streken,

Wiens schelmery en trots : niet syn om uyt te spreken.

Geen grooter booswicht droeg de stad van Golconda.

Deelaghtig aan 'tverraad zyns broers, nooit
wel te vreden,
Heest hy de zelve straf op eenen tyt geleden.

TRANSLATION.

There we see in miniature, the portrait of Akkanna a beast in human form: whose cunning, wicked tricks, whose scoundrelism and pride, should not be uttered (spoken about). No greater villain did the town of Golconda ever witness. Participating in the treason of his brother, he was never contented he suffered the same punishment and at the same time as Mādanna.

D. HAVART.

Tweede deel, Fol. 222=
Second Volume, p. 222.

Madoena en Akkana. Twn gebroeders vermoort, en schandeluk ten tom Gestellt=
Mādanna and Akkanna. Two brothers murdered and scandalously exhibited.

TEXT[1]

श्रीमहादेव ।

१. [स्व]स्ति श्री विजयाम्युदयशालीवाहनशक वंग० ल १६०८

२. [आगुनेटि प्रभवनाम संवत्सरं वशाख[2]शुद्ध १५] स्थिरवा[रं]

1. From inked impressions. 2. Read वैशाख

३. चंद्रोपरागपुण्यकालमंदु [स्वस्ति श्री] मदाखलभ[3] [मंड] ला-
[लं]-
४. कार त्रयास्त्रिंश[त्को]टिदेवताराः[धि]तश्रीकामाक्षीदेवीसनाथ-
५. श्रीमदेकांम्रनाथ श्रामहादेवास[न]ाथ[4] श्राहस्तागिरिनाथसाक्षा-
६. [त्का]र परमाधष्टान[5]सत्यव्रतनामांकितकांचीदिव्यक्षेत्रशा-
७. रदा[म]ठसंस्थितानां[6]मतुलितसुधारसमाधुर्यकमलासन-
८. कामिनीधम्मिल्लसंपुल्ल[7]मल्लिकामालिकानि[ष्यं] दमक-
९. रंदझरीसौवस्थिकवागुंभ[वि]ञंभणा[8]नंदतुंदिलित-
१०. मनी[षी]मंडलाना[9]मनवरताद्वेत[10]विद्या[वि]नोदरासिकानां
११. निरंतरालंकृतीकृतशांतिदांति[भूम्नां] सकलभुवनच[क्र]-
प्रतिष्ठा-
१२. [प][11]काविख्यातयशोलंकृतानां निखि[ल*]पाषंडषंडकंटको-
द्धाटनेन
१३. विशदीकृतवेदवेदांतमार्गप्रतिष्ठापमा[12]चार्याणां श्रीमत्परमहं-
१४. सपरिव्राजकाचा[र्य]श्रीमच्छंकरभगवत्पादाचार्याणामधि[ष्ठा]-
१५. ने सिंहासनाभिषिक्तश्रीमद्चंद्रशेखरेंद्रसरस्वतीसंयमां[13]

---

3. Read मदखिलभू
4. Read देकाम्रनाथश्रीमहादेवी- सनाथश्रीहास्ति
5. Read परमाधिष्ठान
6. Read संस्थितानामतुलित
7. Read संफुल्ल
8. Read सौवस्तिकवागगुम्भवि- जृम्भणा
9. Read मनीषिमण्डलाना
10. Read द्वैत
11. Read प्रतिष्ठापन
12. Read प्रतिष्ठापना
13. Read संयमीन्द्राणा

Inscription of Śaka Samvat, 1608.

SCALE O. 5.

A. GOPINATHA RAO. Half-Tone by Photo-Engraving Co., Madras.

१६. द्राणामंतेवासिवर्यश्रीमहादे[वें]द्रसरस्वतुल चारु (आ)

SECOND SIDE.

१७. आश्वलायनसत्रुलैन वामकायनविश्वामित्र[गो]त्रुलैन

१८. होयसानेकब्रोडवारुरामशास्तुलवारिकि[14] गोलको[*]ड अक्क

१९. न्नमादं[न्न]वारु यिच्चिन तममुसाग्रामंलो चंगलपट्ट[ज्ञा]गीरु

२०. [सी]मल अजूरुदग्गेर मेलुपाकलोनु अग्रहारं चास[15] पनमा-

२१. नसास्थ्यं ऊरिकि उत्तरं च[रु]उकु दक्षिणपु प[श्चि]मद्वि-
मिका १-

२२. व कंण्णारुला[16] तलयीडुकांड्लु आयदुकांड्लु मान्यमुंन्नु
संवत्स-

२३. रानकु मठमुलोनु वरषाशनं २ रेंडु वरहालुंन्नु ानव[श]तं रेंडुं

२४. न्नु आग्रामं लो कनुवडि कलानिकि कानुगोयि देशमुखि मर ३

२५. मूडु अडुलुंनु श्रीचन्द्रमौलीश्वरस्वामिकि मर[अ]नुडुंन्नु यीता-

२६. लुगु अडुंलमगतुंन्नु श्रीचन्द्रमौलीश्वरस्वामिकि अर्पितंगा-

२७. नु दत्तं चेसि दानशासनं व्रासि यिच्चिनामु ॥ श्रीराम ॥-श्री ॥

२८. दानपालनयोर्मध्ये दा [ना]च्छ्रेया[17]नुपालनं दानात्स्वर्गमवा-

२९. प्नोभि पालनादच्युत पद[18] ॥ स्वदत्ता[द्वि]गुणं पुण्यं
परदता[19]-

---

14. Read कर्नाटवारु
15. Read चेसि
16. Read कण्णारुलो
17. Read च्छ्रेयो
18. Read मवाप्नोति पालनाद-
च्युतं पदम्
19. Read द्विगुणं पुण्यं परदत्ता

३०. नुपालनं पर[द]त्ता[प]हारेण [स्व] [द*]त्तं नि[ष्फ]लं
भवेत् ॥ श्री ॥

३१. श्रीचंद्रमौलीश्वरस्वामीसहायं

ABSTRACT OF CONTENTS.[1]

Śrī Mahādēva Sarasvati, the disciple of Śrī Chandraśēkhara Sarasvati, who was an ornament of the world; who belonged to the Śāradā maṭha, which is situated in the divine (city of) Kāñchi, in which are the temples of Ekāmranātha and Kāmākśhi who is adored by the thirty-three crores of gods and of Hastigirinātha and Mahādēvī; who was delighting the crowd of learned men with his nectar-like words, which was sweet as the honey that flows from the wreath of jasmine flowers which adorns the crown of Sarasvatī; who was ever interested in the Advaita-vidya; who was characterised by tranquility and self-control; who, having removed the thorns, namely, the heretic faiths, had established the religion of the Vēdas and Vēdānta; who was consecrated to the seat of the *paramahaṁsa* and *parivrājakāchārya*,—(Mahādēva Sarasvati) granted a copper-plate deed to Rāma Śāstri, of the Hoysaṇa Karnāṭaka sect, belonging

---

(1) The document is not wholly intelligible.

Ib

Inscription of Śaka Samvat, 1608.

SCALE O. 5.

T. A. GOPINATHA RAO. Half-Tone by Photo-Engraving Co., Madras.

to Vāmkāyan Viśwāmittra Gotra. It was the year 1930.

Between the protection of charity and the giving of it, the former is of greater merit than the latter. By gift one attains Svarga only which is transient whereas by the latter one attains the eternal bliss, which is imperishable one.

Sri Chandramaulishwar Swami be the protector!